Cartoons and Comics in the Classroom

CARTOONS AND COMICS
IN THE CLASSROOM

A Reference for
Teachers and Librarians

Edited with a preface by
James L. Thomas

1983

Libraries Unlimited, Inc.
Littleton, Colorado

LIBRARIES UNLIMITED, INC.
P.O. Box 263
Littleton, Colorado 80160

Library of Congress Cataloging in Publication Data

Main entry under title:

Cartoons and comics in the classroom.

    Bibliography: p. 167
    Includes index.
    1. Comic books, strips, etc. in education--Handbooks,
manuals, etc. I. Thomas, James L., 1945-
LB1044.9.C59C37 1983   371.3'2   82-17957
ISBN 0-87287-357-9

Libraries Unlimited books are bound with Type II nonwoven material that meets
and exceeds National Association of State Textbook Administrators' Type II
nonwoven material specifications Class A through E.

TABLE OF CONTENTS

PREFACE

Most of us who have taught either children or young adults have at one time or another encountered these young people entranced by cartoons in a newspaper column or reacting to the superheroes of a comic book. Too often our immediate responses have been to remove, restrain, or inhibit such materials, especially in the classroom. Why? For many, cartoons and comics reflect the worst possible literature — stereotyping of characters; inferior, idiomatic writing; weak, canned plot structure; etc. Others, however, have discovered value and have benefitted from using this medium in instruction. Many have written about the motivational factors they have experienced with cartoons and comics as a part of their curriculum. This compilation chronicles the ways in which these professionals have utilized both comics and cartoons over the past ten years with students.

The text begins with a general introduction for the background of the reader and is followed by four major sections asking the questions: where? how? when? and with whom? cartoons and/or comics might be used. The articles in each section answer the individual questions. An annotated bibliography for further reference concludes the work.

— James L. Thomas

CONTRIBUTORS

HOWARD G. BALL is Professor, School Library Media, Alabama A&M University at Normal. "Who Is Snoopy?" is reprinted by permission of *Language Arts* (October 1976, vol. 53, pp. 798-802). Copyright © 1976 by the National Council of Teachers of English.

BRUCE BROCKA is a master's degree student at the University of Iowa and lives in Tucson, Arizona. "Comic Books — In Case You Haven't Noticed They've Changed" is reprinted by permission of *Media & Methods* (May/June 1979, vol. 15, pp. 30-32).

CHRISTIAN BRÜGGEMANN is Director of Studies at a German college in Wiesbaden, West Germany. "Comic Strips in the Teaching of English as a Foreign Language" by Christian Brüggemann and Robert J. Elkins is an ERIC Document (ED 056 591) and is in the public domain.

DR. CLARENCE R. CALDER, JR., is a Professor of Education in the School of Education, University of Connecticut, Storrs. "Cartoon Characters in the Language Arts" by Clarence Calder and Julie Carlson McAlpine is reprinted by permission of *Elementary English* (October 1972, vol. 49, pp. 853-56). Copyright © 1972 by the National Council of Teachers of English.

ANN CARLYLE is a teacher in the Goleta Union School District in Goleta, California. "Comic Book Club" is reprinted by special permission of *Learning* (April 1978, vol. 6, p. 48), The Magazine for Creative Teaching, April 1978. Copyright © 1978 by Pitman Learning, Inc.

DR. CHARLES E. CARRAHER, JR., is Chairman, Department of Chemistry, Wright State University in Dayton, Ohio. "Comics: No-Nonsense Classroom Aids" is reprinted by permission of *Science Teacher* (November 1975, vol. 42, p. 30). Copyright © 1975 by National Science Teachers Association.

DR. C. EDWARD CARROLL is Professor of Library and Information Science at the University of Missouri — Columbia. "Spider-Man at the Library" by Larry Dorrell and Ed Carroll is reprinted with permission from

School Library Journal (August 1981, vol. 27, pp. 17-19). R. R. Bowker Co./A Xerox Corporation.

MARK COHAN is author of "Comic Books in the Classroom." The article is reprinted with permission of the National Council for the Social Studies from *Social Education* (May 1975, vol. 39, pp. 324-25).

ALEX DOBROWOLSKI teaches at Franklin High School in Somerset, New Jersey. "The Comic Book Is Alive and Well and Living in the History Class" is used by permission of *Social Studies* (May/June 1976, vol. 67, pp. 118-20). Copyright © 1976 by Heldref Publications, 4000 Albemarle St., NW, Washington, DC 20016.

DR. LARRY D. DORRELL is Media Director, West Junior High School, Columbia, Missouri. "Spider-Man at the Library" by Larry Dorrell and Ed Carroll is reprinted with permission from *School Library Journal* (August 1981, vol. 27, pp. 17-19). R. R. Bowker Co./A Xerox Corporation.

ROBERT J. ELKINS is Chairman and Professor of German, Department of Foreign Languages, West Virginia University, Morgantown. "Comic Strips in the Teaching of English as a Foreign Language" by Robert J. Elkins and Christian Brüggemann is an ERIC Document (ED 056 591) and is in the public domain.

NEIL ELLMAN is Assistant Superintendent in the Hanover Park Regional High School District, Hanover, New Jersey. "Comics in the Classroom" is reprinted by permission of *Audiovisual Instruction* (May 1979, vol. 24, pp. 24-25), Association for Educational Communications and Technology.

PHYLLIS N. HALLENBECK, Ph.D., is Director, Hallenbeck Psycho-Educational Center in Willoughby, Ohio. "Remediating with Comic Strips" is reprinted by permission of *Journal of Learning Disabilities* (January 1976, vol. 9, pp. 22-26).

WILLIAM RAY HEITZMANN teaches in the Department of Political Science at Villanova University in Pennsylvania. "The Political Cartoon as a Teaching Device" is reprinted by permission of *Teaching Political Science* (January 1979, vol. 6, pp. 166-84). Copyright © 1979 by Sage Publications.

ROBINETTE CURRY HOOVER is the author of "Language for the Deaf According to *Henry*." The article is reprinted by permission of *American Annals of the Deaf* (December 1974, vol. 119, pp. 590-94).

JILL KAISERMAN is the author of "Comprehension through Comics." The article is reprinted by special permission of *Learning* (March 1979, vol. 7, p. 64), The Magazine for Creative Teaching, March 1979. Copyright © 1979 by Pitman Learning, Inc.

HERBERT KOHL is the author of "Origins: Where Did I Come From? Where Am I Going?" The article is reprinted by permission of *Teacher* (March 1977, vol. 94, pp. 12, 14). Copyright © by Herbert R. Kohl.

JULIE CARLSON McALPINE is affiliated with the Newport School Department in Newport, Rhode Island. "Cartoon Characters in the Language Arts" by Clarence Calder and Julie Carlson McAlpine is reprinted by permission of *Elementary English* (October 1972, vol. 49, pp. 853-56). Copyright © 1972 by the National Council of Teachers of English.

RUFUS K. MARSH is a lecturer at the University of Evansville in Indiana. "Teaching French with Comics" is reprinted by permission of *French Review* (May 1976, vol. 51, pp. 777-85).

DORIS P. MILLER is English Department Head at Rutland Junior High in Rutland, Vermont. "Cartoon Kits" is reprinted by special permission of *Learning* (February 1978, vol. 6, p. 112), The Magazine for Creative Teaching. Copyright © 1978 by Pitman Learning, Inc. "A Student-Made Filmstrip" is reprinted by permission of *Media & Methods* (September 1975, vol. 12, p. 18).

ELFRIEDA C. PIERCE is a sixth grade English instructor at Lenox Memorial Middle School, Lenox, Massachusetts. "Word Study: Comic Strip Style" is reprinted by special permission of *Learning* (November 1977, vol. 6, p. 48), The Magazine for Creative Teaching, November 1977. Copyright © 1977 by Pitman Learning, Inc.

RON RAINSBURY is author of "Where Is Droopy?" The article is reprinted by permission of *Arithmetic Teacher* (April 1972, vol. 19, pp. 271-72). Copyright © 1972 by the National Council of Teachers of Mathematics.

DR. JUNE ROSE RICHIE is Assistant Professor of Curriculum and Instruction at Memphis State University, Memphis, Tennessee. "The Funnnies Aren't Just Funny.... Using Cartoons and Comics to Teach" is reprinted by permission of *The Clearing House* (November 1979, vol. 53, pp. 125-28). Copyright © 1979 by Heldref Publications, 4000 Albemarle St., NW, Washington, DC 20016.

MAURICE K. SCHIFFMAN is the author of "Science Cartoons." The article is reproduced with permission from *Science and Children* (November/December 1977, vol. 15, p. 46). Copyright © 1977 by the National Science Teachers Association, 1742 Connecticut Avenue, NW, Washington, DC 20009.

ROBERT N. SCHOOF, JR., is a teacher with the Monroe Public Schools in Monroe, Michigan. "Four-Color Words: Comic Books in the Classroom" is reprinted by permission of *Language Arts* (October 1978, vol. 55, pp. 821-27). Copyright © 1978 by the National Council of Teachers of English.

FRANK W. SOSNOWSKI is author of "Report Making—The Cartoon Way." The article is reprinted from *Teacher* (March 1975, vol. 92, pp. 75-77). Copyright © by Macmillan Professional Magazines. Used by permission of The Instructor Publications, Inc.

BILL STARK is Director of Media Services, Illinois School for the Deaf in Jacksonville. " 'Meanwhile ... ': A Look at Comic Books at Illinois School for the Deaf" is reprinted by permission of *American Annals of the Deaf* (October 1976, vol. 121, pp. 470-77).

EMMA HALSTEAD SWAIN is Assistant Professor of Reading Education at West Virginia College of Graduate Studies, Institute, West Virginia. "Using Comic Books to Teach Reading and Language Arts" is reprinted by permission of Emma H. Swain and and International Reading Association from *Journal of Reading* (December 1978, vol. 22, pp. 253-58).

DAVID C. ULMER, JR., is a doctoral candidate at the University of Nebraska—Lincoln and a science instructor at William Mitchell High School in Colorado Springs, Colorado. "Cartoon Schooling" is reprinted by permission of *Science Teacher* (May 1978, vol. 45, p. 44).

TRUDY URBANI is a teacher in the Bedford Public Schools, Temperance, Michigan. "Fun, Funny, Funnies" is reprinted from *Teacher* (September 1978, vol. 96, pp. 60-62, 64, 66, 68). Copyright © by Macmillan Professional Magazines. Used by permission of The Instructor Publications, Inc.

NEIL VAIL is Director, Reading/Language Arts K-12 with the Racine Unified School District in Wisconsin. "English Create from Cartoons" is reprinted from *Instructor* (January 1975, vol. 84, pp. 51-52). Copyright © by The Instructor Publications, Inc. Used by permission.

GARY WRIGHT is Professor of Education, University of Texas at Tyler. "The Comic Strip in the Classroom for the Reluctant Disabled Reader" is reprinted by permission of *Reading Improvement* (Spring 1979, vol. 16, pp. 13-17). Copyright © 1979 by Project Innovation, 1362 Santa Cruz Court, Chula Vista, CA 92010. "The Comic Book—A Forgotten Medium in the Classroom" is reprinted with permission of Gary Wright and the International Reading Association from *The Reading Teacher* (November 1979, vol. 33, pp. 158-61).

INTRODUCTION

- what the comic strip has to offer educators and education

- reasons for utilizing the comic book in the classroom

- how comics have changed over the years

- the value of using the comic book medium with students

WHO IS SNOOPY?   Howard G. Ball

To ask this question today is like asking who is 'Tania' Hearst? The American comic strip is one of the great reflectors of this nation's culture. Comic materials reflect our culture's happier as well as our joyless moments. Comic strips portray our national weaknesses as well as our strengths. Cynicism, satire, dishonesty, wit, humor, and yes, even facts are presented through this medium.

Originally, the comic strip was designed to carry visual messages to many non-reading migrants who had recently entered this nation. The messages of this medium were often indoctrinating in that they attempted to persuade the newcomer to accept a particular issue, honor a specific event, or support ideologies revered by the majority of this society. It was an effective medium for perpetuating the values and mores that were considered important for the growth of this country. An example of this assimilating effort was reflected through Bud Fisher's characterizations of "Mutt and Jeff," the archetypes of the earlier work-ethic philosophy. This series presented to the uninitiated comic audience a succession of pictorial activities that graphically demonstrated the qualities of personal achievement and lifestyles of the rapidly emerging middle-class society. The rewards for belonging to this growing stratum were presented in vivid detail.

It was during the middle 1920's that comic materials expanded into an entertainment medium. Humorous situations were injected into the content of comic strips. In addition, these strips provided an emotional release for much of America's reading public. Whatever it is that makes this medium so effective — humor, escape, or the appeal to the basic human emotions — the comics have it, and they seem to have more of it than parents and teachers even suspect.

Many educators and parents have presented highly vocal arguments opposing the use of comic materials. Educators and parents seem to view comic strips as trite and promiscuous media; media that have little or no intellectual integrity and detract from the quality of instructional stateliness.

Although research has done little to prove or disprove any adverse effects that comic materials could have upon the attitudes and behaviors of readers, the following are some of the criticisms directed at this medium:

- Too often comic materials present personal violence and crime as the focal part of the content.

- Comic materials depicting interpersonal violence increase aggressive behaviors of the readers.

- Not only are focal points of personal violence and crime the major content, but details of crimes, and other types of antisocial behaviors, are demonstrated.

- Comics presenting undesirable content can distort the readers' values and attitudes, their opinions and beliefs.

- Diversity in content is lacking. The roles of the characters are stereotyped and the plots are stylized. Publishers seem reluctant to change their "proven" and "tested" themes.

- Comics present white male characters largely in roles of leadership and position of centrality. Women and children are usually shown in positions of passivity and domesticity, mostly supporting the white male characters.

- Minorities are seldom represented in proportion to the nation's population, and when presented, they are seldom assigned positions of respect and prestige.

- Publishers of comic materials have extended little effort to assess how their materials are affecting the perceptions and behaviors of readers.

Even as we reject and denounce the use of comic books, children and adults are buying, reading and thoroughly enjoying the "funnies." These readers have even claimed they are gaining important information from these materials. If comic materials can increase negative and aggressive attitudes and behaviors on the part of their readers, then they conceivably can encourage other types of human behaviors. Researchers are finding indications that socially accepted behaviors can be communicated through the "funnies" medium.

No question about it, comic materials are one of the most widely read media in this country. To reject all comics as intellectually repressive and aesthetically void is an apology for shallowness, masquerading as intellectual sophistication.

As users of a variety of instructional materials, we might address ourselves to the following questions:

- How have other teachers utilized comic materials?

- Have I identified, or attempted to identify, any comic materials that have instructional value?

- Have I ever made an effort to investigate the value of comic materials?

- Have I asked my learners what they enjoy about comics?

- Have I recently taken time to examine a representative sample of the comic materials available in my community?

- Have I read comics, and if so, did I enjoy them?

- Have I recently read any published studies or critiques for or against the use of comic materials in the classroom?

- To what extent do my learners read comic materials outside of my classroom?

- Are children really engaged in a legitimate act of reading while addressing their attending behaviors to comic materials?

- Are there any comic materials available that could be used to complement my instructional efforts?

- What is my school system's policy for using comic materials in the classroom?

- What are the opinions and attitudes of laypersons in this community on the use of comic books as an instructional tool?

The comic strip was originally created to provide a lower-level form of communication and amusement. It was considered a chronicle of ignobility. But today, this is not the case. Comics appeal to all levels of American society. Comic materials enjoy a higher readership than any other print-oriented medium, except the daily newspaper, and interestingly, the newspaper is a medium that includes comic materials as a featured part of its presentation.

In addition to their entertainment objective, comics are being used by: 1) businesses and industries to convey corporate activities and programs; 2) local, state, and federal agencies to promote a variety of public service issues affecting the physical, social, emotional, and psychological well-being of their citizens; 3) commercial publications to provide information on vocational and career opportunities; and 4) manufacturers of equipment to demonstrate steps and procedures for operating and maintaining equipment. These are but a few of the responsible communicative tasks now being charged to the comic medium.

Recent estimates of the mass appeal of comic materials indicate that comics are read by more than one hundred thirty million Americans each week. Can we as educators really afford to neglect a medium that attracts and motivates such a large readership?

It has been posited by many critics of comic materials that this medium portrays violence, murder, corruption, dishonesty, inhumane treatment, terror, sadism, and destruction—to name but a few of the afflictions that plague society. At this point, we might ask ourselves what medium displays or presents these afflictions with less intensity. Our daily newspapers are riddled with the distortions and disorders of society. National television develops its prime-time shows around the same illicit conditions and outrages that torment our nation's communities. Hardcover and paperback books present coercion and passion in such vivid and languished terms that little is left for the reader to reflect on or to contemplate. Why then are we so critical of comic materials when they display the same themes and improprieties as all of the other popular mass media?

Unlike the other popular media, comic materials did not begin with a substantive base. The comic book has never enjoyed the scholarliness of the printed book. Historically, it has not been the recorder or the heralder of man's progress, growth and development. Comic materials have not had the opportunities to store and then present the philosophies, tenets and ideologies of mankind, nor been privileged with the high speed and dynamic communication qualities of the electronic media. Neither have comics contained the day to day information necessary for man's cultural, economic, and political survival as has the daily newspaper.

Unfortunately, the comic strip started as a vehicle for propaganda, a ledger for buffoonery. It has been difficult for the comic medium, regardless of any potential properties, to rise above the level of literal commonality.

A medium that is to become effective and communicate to the public must mirror the immediate culture. This is a valid criterion for any successful medium. This reflection is necessary if readers are to interpret, in a meaningful way, the plot, signs, and symbols used to communicate the message. It is also necessary that the medium offer some familiarity of incidents or experiences with which the reader can identify and relate. A study of the evolution of comic materials demonstrated that they have done an extraordinary job of mirroring the events and issues of the day. The Blondie comic series presents middleclass values and mores with such candor and realism that the series is rated as the number one comic item in this country; and in many foreign countries also. The frustrations, insecurities, pressures, demands and other adjustment problems in this society are portrayed in Peanuts. As the priorities and foci for crime on society, along with systems of crime detection, have changed, so as the Dick Tracy series changed. Decades ago, Dick Tracy spent months and months tracking down one elusive clue after another in order to solve a baffling case. Today he uses modern electronic detection techniques that make him the "super" detective of all detectives.

Yes, popular comics do reflect contemporary society. In many cases they are not just passive reflectors but formative channels for change. The social activist defenders of civilized values seen in "Doonesbury" aim to point out areas for change and give prescriptions for implementing change.

The comic strip has proven to be an exceptional communicative device. It uses a language common to most members of this society. It presents a written text that augments the visual form. Visual forms are often presented with such pictorial quality and clarity of image that the fidelity of the communicated message is superior to many other media using similar visual/verbal displays.

An effective comic strip develops its plot in a sequential fashion, with visual displays moving from left to right on the comic page. As ideas and understandings are developed for readers, they become more involved thoughtfully and emotionally. For instance, as Dagwood becomes more and more frustrated and pressured in his continuous attempt to survive in his oppressive environment, so do the readers laud and applaud his hopeless efforts. Lucy and Charlie Brown are personifications of the internal struggles and rivalries which frustrate us. The readers relate to these incidents and demand continued expansion of this subtle and sophisticated strip.

Research points out that most readers of comic materials enjoy them for their "fun" aspects. Comics are a pleasant and relaxing way to pass the time. Since comic materials can be enjoyed by individuals or groups, dynamically interacting and sharing the printed thoughts and expressions—they have demonstrated their potential value in almost any type of instructional setting.

Comic materials, as any other instructional medium, must be judiciously selected. There are comic materials to suit the needs and interests of all types of readers.

Assertions have been made that comic materials reflect and reinforce our social system, affect readers' opinions and attitudes, and provide a vehicle for acculturation for each succeeding generation. If these assertions can be accepted, then educators need to develop some awareness of how comic materials are being used to influence.

Educators, and parents, too, can influence children's uses of comic materials. They can establish standards which affect the kinds of materials children select. They can assert themselves with publishers of materials for children. If readers become familiar with the influencing powers of comic materials, the kinds of information presented, and the techniques used to present the information, they would be in a better position to discern how comic materials influence their lives. If a comic strip is clearly designed for promoting a particular ideology or principle, adults should assist the reader to discern the message and put it in perspective.

Comics cannot generically be considered either important or unimportant. A comic medium must be selected in terms of the effects it will have upon the learning behaviors of a particular group of readers. Another important consideration in selecting appropriate comic materials is how the material can assist in the attainment of the instructional goals or objectives.

In determining the instructional appropriateness of a particular comic, the following standards may be applied:

1. The content of the comic material would not adversely distort the attitudes or opinions of the readers.

2. The pictures provide the readers with experiences for interpreting complex and detailed information.

3. The printed text and the pictures can be interpreted and read by those with whom the materials will be used.

4. The pictorial images are representative of things, situations, or places familiar to the reader.

5. The characters in the materials would appeal to and be of interest to those readers with whom the materials are to be used.

6. Abstract ideas, or symbolic images are presented in a manner that can readily be perceived by the readers.

7. The colors used enhance and give the pictures a lifelike, dynamic quality.

8. The material displays a continuity of action.

9. The printed text is intelligible and suitably organized.

10. The overall format of the material is attractive and pleasing to the eye.

11. The words and pictures complement each other and collectively present the same message.

12. The material provides pleasant, active, learner-oriented activities.

13. The cost of the material does not seem excessive when considering its instructional value.

14. The material realistically represents the characters and incidents.

15. The content is designed to motivate the reader to continue through to the conclusion of the story.

16. The understandings, concepts, awarenesses, and issues as presented are displayed in an organized and sequential manner.

17. The ideas and pictures are not offensive to any readers with whom the material would be used.

18. The concepts presented within the content of the material do not conflict with acceptable dogmas, principles, tenets, or beliefs of the immediate culture.

19. The content of the material leads to or suggests other related media sources or activities that the reader might use in gaining additional knowledge about a particular issue, concept, or topic.

20. The material would provide worthwhile experiences and understandings for the readers.

The proper presentation of a successful comic strip requires thoughtful planning; an understanding of the content to be presented; and a planned and organized way for collecting, arranging and presenting information.

Comic materials are effectively being used in a variety of instructional settings. They can help to meet the educational needs of learners. Whether we choose to use them or not is of no consequence for the future of this medium. Comic materials have been smuggled into our classrooms for years. Do we now have the skills to use them wisely?

References

Andrews, Mildred B. "Comic Books Are Serious Aids to Community Education." *Textile World* (May 1953): 53-59.

Ball, Howard G. "The Adventures of Captain Media." *Library Scene* (June 1975): 16-20.

_____. "Pictorial Assessment and Selection." *Audiovisual Instruction* (January 1975): 20-26.

White, David M. and Abel, Robert H. *The Funnies: An American Idiom.* London: Collier-Macmillan Ltd., 1963.

THE COMIC BOOK –
A FORGOTTEN MEDIUM IN THE CLASSROOM

Gary Wright

The comic book has been a part of American culture since 1933 – four and one-half decades. Weekly and Sunday comic strips have been around for twice that time, in newspapers in many different countries and languages.

Indeed, the comics have endured because they have interested and excited child, adolescent and adult alike. Line, color and print on the comic page interact, first to attract the eye and then to draw the mind into a world of fantasy and fun.

The comic book has provided satisfying leisure reading for millions of children throughout the world. In spite of this, there is a paucity of articles on comics in educational literature. Knowledge about this source of classroom reading material may help the teacher in using it wisely.

Children's Interest in Comics

As reading teachers we must recognize the fact that comics appeal to large numbers of children and that such an appeal is normal. Let's look at the facts. Sinkovec, Tiefenbacher and Finger (1978) listed 113 different children's comic book titles released to U.S. newsstands during June 1978. Most of these titles have a monthly press run exceeding 50,000 copies. Millions of comic books distributed and purchased annually attest to children's interest in the medium.

Studies on children's reading interests during the past four decades support the fact that children enjoy reading comics. Dechant and Smith (1977) have summarized research studies on children's reading interests which indicate that the comic book is popular with primary, intermediate and junior high students. Popularity of the comic book increases throughout the elementary school years and peaks among 12 to 14 year olds. Though many high school and college age students read comics, the major consumers seem to be children between the ages of 9 and 13.

Reprinted with permission of the author and the International Reading Association from *Reading Teacher* 33 (November 1979): 158-61.

Who Creates Comics?

There are five major publishers of comic books in the U.S. which are appropriate for classroom use. The following is a list of these publishers and a brief description of the kinds of comics each distributes. Readers in other countries can perhaps obtain similar information either from magazine dealers or their own students.

Archie Comic Publications. Publishes humorous comic books about Archie and his teenage friends.

D.C. Comics, Inc. Specializes in adventure, mystery, romance, western and war comics. D.C. Comics is known for its superheroes and superheroines, i.e., Batman, Superman and Wonder Woman.

Harvey Publications, Inc. Specializes in humor. Casper the Friendly Ghost and Sad Sack are two of the company's major titles.

Marvel Comics Group, Inc. Distributes adventure, mystery, romance, cowboy and war titles. This company specializes in superheroes such as Spiderman, Captain America and the Hulk.

Western Publishing Company. This company publishes Gold Key Comics, which feature funny animal characters such as Bugs Bunny, Donald Duck, Mickey Mouse, Mighty Mouse and Woody Woodpecker.

Quality of Comic Books

Comic books are graphic stories written primarily for children and adolescents. Generally, the stories contain all the elements of short stories: characters, dialogue, plot, conflict and climax. By no stretch of the imagination can comic book stories be called great literature. However, most comic book publishers are interested in the quality of their product and most ascribe to the Comics Code Authority (Daniels 1971).

The Comics Code Authority is an organization which has set up an elaborate list of restrictions with which all subscribing publishers are expected to comply. Compliance with the code is rewarded by allowing comic book publishers to display a seal on comic book covers, "Approved by the Comics Code Authority."

The code sets standards for comic book writers and artists. It covers both editorial and advertising matter, concerning the topics of characterization, costumes, dialogue, plot, marriage, religion, sex, violence, and vocabulary.

The purpose of the code is to assure parents that the material within the comic is reasonably wholesome. The publishers listed earlier abide by the code. However, there are publishing companies which do not. If in doubt about an American comic book title, look for the comic code seal on the cover.

Code standards have helped improve the quality of comics, and the people who create comics are also helping to bring quality to the medium. Today, the scriptwriters, artists and editors of comic books are highly literate professionals, most of whom have graduated from colleges and art schools.

Readability of Comics

Comic book readability is a pioneer area for research. I have conducted a preliminary study on the readability levels of 20 popular comic book titles. The extended Fry Readability Graph (Fry 1977) and the Maginnis Extended Fry Readability Graph (Maginnis 1969) were used for the readability estimates presented in the Table. Three samples, each 100 words in length, were taken from the comic books listed.

The average readability of these comic books ranges from 1.8 to 6.4 grade level. Obviously, the difficulty level is such that most first and second grade students would not be attracted to them as a source of recreational reading.

READABILITY LEVELS OF 20 COMIC BOOKS

Title	Readability grade level of 3 samples	Average readability level
The Amazing Spiderman #187 (Dec. 1978)	7.4, 3.0, 2.8	4.4
Archie #274 (Sept. 1978)	2.0, 1.7, 1.7	1.8
Batman #299 (May 1978)	7.9, 4.0, 8.5	6.4
Bugs Bunny #201 (Oct. 1978)	2.9, 1.9, 1.7	2.1
Casper the Friendly Ghost #200 (Oct. 1978)	1.9, 1.7, 1.7	1.8
Chip and Dale #55 (Nov. 1978)	2.9, 1.9, 1.8	2.2
Dennis the Menace #158 (July 1978)	1.4, 1.5, 1.7	1.5
Donald Duck #201 (Nov. 1978)	2.8, 3.0, 4.7	3.5
Incredible Hulk #74 (Nov. 1978)	5.5, 9.2, 1.9	5.5
Mighty Mouse #53 (Nov. 1978)	1.9, 3.3, 1.9	2.4
Sad Sack #265 (Nov. 1978)	2.4, 1.9, 1.9	2.1
Spidey Super Stories #37 (Nov. 1978)	2.7, 1.8, 1.9	2.1
Star Hunters #7 (Nov. 1978)	6.0, 7.3, 3.3	5.5
Star Wars #16 (Oct. 1978)	7.5, 7.4, 3.3	6.1
Superman #329 (Nov. 1978)	7.3, 8.3, 3.5	6.4
Tarzan #18 (Nov. 1978)	7.6, 4.4, 4.5	5.5
Tom and Jerry #311 (Oct. 1978)	1.9, 2.0, 1.8	1.9
Wonder Woman #245 (July 1978)	5.5, 5.5, 3.5	4.8
Woody Woodpecker #172 (Nov. 1978)	2.4, 2.4, 3.0	3.1
Yogi Bear #7 (Nov. 1978)	3.2, 3.5, 2.4	3.0

However, average and above average readers in the intermediate and junior high grades would find most comic books easy to read.

Humorous and funny animal comics tend to have lower readability levels than the superhero comics. Also, the range of readability within the humorous and funny animal comics is less than that of superhero comics. All superhero comics listed in the Table had an internal readability range of three grade levels or more. In view of the wide range of readability levels among comic books, one cannot assume that all comic books are easy to read.

Comics in the Classroom

Publishers of educational materials are beginning to recognize the potential of comics in the classroom. For example, Holt, Rinehart and Winston (383 Madison Avenue, New York, New York 10017) has published *The Super Dictionary* (1978), a beginner's dictionary illustrated with Superman, Batman, Wonder Woman and other superheroes. Science Research Associates (155 N. Wacker Dr., Chicago, Illinois 60606) has Super Kits for reluctant readers which use comic books to provide reading practice. King Features Syndicate (Education Division, 235 East 45th Street, New York, New York 10017) has published comics for use in language, reading and career awareness programs.

Several writers have described the benefits of using comics in the classroom. Burton (1961), Murphy (1961), Haugaard (1973) and Alongi (1974) have related the motivational value of comic books. Each writer agreed that comic books turned children on to reading, and that comic books had much to offer as a source of recreational reading.

One research study does point out an area of caution for teachers using comic books. Arlin and Roth (1978) report that when third graders were given free time for comics, the good readers spent their time actually reading but the poor readers mostly just looked at the pictures (they spent only 24% of their time on the words). This points up two things for the teacher. First, we must not assume that comic books are primarily motivators for slower students; they are most effective with able readers. Second, we must take steps to ensure that the poorer readers stay on task.

Classroom teachers should not forget comic books. Children's interest in them has not dissipated during the last half century; if anything, it has increased. It is in the reading teacher's best interest to learn more about this medium and to use it in motivating students and helping them to read.

References

Alongi, Constance V. "Response to Kay Haugaard Comic Books Revisited." *The Reading Teacher*, vol. 27, no. 8 (May 1974), pp. 801-03.

Arlin, Marshall and Garry Roth. "Pupils' Use of Time While Reading Comics and Books." *American Educational Research Journal*, vol. 15, no. 2 (Spring 1978), pp. 201-16.

Burton, Dwight L. "Campaigning to Get Students to Read." *Reading in the Secondary Schools*. M. Jerry Weiss, Ed., pp. 186-87. New York, N.Y.: The Odyssey Press, 1961.

Daniels, Les. *Comix: A History of Comic Books in America*. pp. 83-90. New York, N.Y.: Bonanza Books, 1971.

Dechant Emerald V. and Henry P. Smith. *Psychology in Teaching Reading*. pp. 182-86. Englewood Cliffs, N.J.: Prentice-Hall, 1977.

Fry, Edward. "Fry's Readability Graph Clarifications, Validity and Extension to Level 17." *Journal of Reading*, vol. 21, no. 3 (December 1977), pp. 242-52.

Haugaard, Kay. "Comic Books Conduits to Culture?" *The Reading Teacher*, vol. 27, no. 1 (October 1973), pp. 54-55.

Maginnis, George H. "The Readability Graph and Informal Reading Inventories." *The Reading Teacher*, vol. 22, no. 6 (March 1969), pp. 516-28, 559.

Murphy, George E. "Some Start with Comics." *Reading in the Secondary Schools*. M. Jerry Weiss, Ed., pp. 186-87. New York, N.Y.: The Odyssey Press, 1961.

Sinkovec, Jerome L., Michael Tiefenbacher and David Finger. *The Comic Reader*, vol. 1, no. 157 (June 1978), p. 15.

COMIC BOOKS: IN CASE YOU HAVEN'T NOTICED THEY'VE CHANGED

Bruce Brocka

When it comes to reading, we want to give students something that will bring 'em back alive, something that will appeal to all levels and tastes. By comparing recent test scores to those of past years, it is easy to see that we have failed somewhere along the line to do this. The curriculum needs a hero — maybe even a superhero — to help it out. But what could possibly provide the action and interest that would arouse this generation of hesitant readers from their addiction to the non-stop action of television? What literary medium might compete with the graphic power of TV? How about comic books?

Comic books???? You've got to be kidding! What would parents say? We already have specially-prepared texts — aren't they adequate, and more appropriate?

All of these questions seem justified. But let's not be too hasty in relegating comic books to the junk heap. They just may be a legitimate classroom resource, especially if we combine them with other activities and media.

To understand how comic books got such a bleak reputation, it's important to take a look at their history. When comics grew up — in the forties — there were no standards of quality or censorship. Violence and gross ethnic and racial slurs (all of which are banned today) were common lures for the bubble-gum crowd's dime. In those days, comics looked like they had been created by crazed cranks who learned the trade in prison or on the streets. Only a few were rendered with skill — Superman, Batman, Captain America — and they're the ones that survived.

During the fifties, when the public was scrutinizing everything from comics to commies, comic book publishers felt the (well-deserved) assault. Doom seemed so imminent that they established a set of guidelines for themselves. Writers and artists, in an attempt to "clean up their act," began to grind out boring and repetitive stories about spooks and funny animals. Heroics sagged into a comatose state. Gone were the days of Brobdingnagian spectacles. The guidelines, which were intended to provide a frame of reference, instead created a stagnant vacuum in which the comic book was slowly dying.

In 1961 a "Marvel-ous" phenomenon occurred: the creation of the Fantastic Four. A few years later, Spiderman, Thor, Hulk, The Avengers, Iron Man and Captain America appeared on the scene. Marvel Comics had a plethora of new heroes and avid new fans. Almost all of these heroes were the invention of one man — Stan Lee — then a writer and now the publisher of Marvel Comics. Tired of

Reprinted by permission of the author and *Media & Methods* 15 (May/June 1979): 30-32.

churning out trite science fiction and fantasy stories for a yawning audience, Lee decided to give comic books a shot in the arm. The result was an innovative philosophy which pervaded not only Marvel comics (see *Marvel's Greatest Superhero Battles*, $6.95, Simon and Schuster) but most of their competitors—including DC, the publisher of Superman, Batman and The Justice League.

What was this philosophy? The basic ingredients were still there: heroes, villains, action, fantastic plots, astounding inventions and gizmos. But the new ingredient was realism. This combination made comics the equal of other creative media.

Lee added depth to his characters, treating them as though they were real beings with real problems—the kind we all face every day. His heroes suffered identity crises, had trouble keeping their love relationships intact, and struggled to convince a skeptical society of their good intentions. The idiosyncrasies and personal lives of these superheroes were woven into the subplots, and sometimes provided the basis for the plot itself.

In addition to their personal problems—and always within the context of their crusade against the forces of evil—the superheroes were embroiled in the leading cultural and social issues of the times. In a word, comics became relevant. Fresh directions were also taken in terms of continuous and coherent stories: plots no longer suffered from overuse. Villains were repeat offenders and the more they appeared, the more their characterization developed. In fact, several "baddies" became so popular that entire comic books were devoted to them.

Comic book quality was improved by aiming at an older audience—junior high through college. Veteran artists and writers moved to greener pastures; new ones were trained by apprenticeship or in colleges. Many who began as fans now produce the comics that grew out of Stan Lee's original philosophy.

All right, so comic books are now created with good intentions. But are they preferable to texts made specifically for secondary classroom use? Are the elements in comics more suitable for arousing student interest and expanding student perception? Maybe.

Comics are a dynamic combination of visual image and written word, of narrative and dialogue. They have just the cohesive and choreographed imagery we need to reach our students. Also, the great variety and periodicity of comic books make them a viable tool. Any pre-teen can cope with the language of Spiderman; on the other hand, the vernacular and prose of Dr. Strange and Warlock would be a challenge for many high school and college students. Not only does the vocabulary level of comics vary—so does their conceptual level. And finally, there's the easy accessibility and low cost of comics—what other teaching resource can you buy at the local supermarket for forty cents a crack?

And now that you are (hopefully) willing to try comics, how do you use them? Obviously, comics are a part of the popular culture and could be studied for what they reveal about contemporary lifestyles, myths, and values. But if you're feeling a little more daring—or desperate—you might try a unit on comics as part of your language arts or media studies curriculum.

Like other literary forms, comics are useful for an analysis of such things as plot and character development; they have the added advantage of using pictures to carry the story along or tell us what kind of person the hero or villain is. Indeed, an interesting activity—suggested by Bill Berhardt in *Just Writing* (Teachers and Writers Collaborative, $4.00)—is to provide the frames from a section of a comic book, but with the words removed, and let the students create a story line or a dialogue.

Literary devices that are the tools-in-trade of the renowned and respectable authors also turn up in comics. Most any comic book will have examples of foreshadowing, irony, setting, stereotyping, flashback—the list is almost endless. Satire is a particular favorite of comic book creators. Not only do the superhero magazines poke fun, but comics in the tradition of *Mad* magazine have honed this technique to a sharp edge. When the spoof is aimed at a literary word (*Mad's* "The Carterbury Tales," for example), it opens the door to the characteristics of the form, and could lead students to an interest in the original work. The satirizing of popular phenomena (TV programs, current fads, movies) can often provide an insight that is missed when we view the genuine item.

Media studies is another area that could benefit by including comics. With their usual ratio of a hundred panels of artwork to twenty pages of writing, comics are about as visual a form as you can get and still be considered "print." The tie-in with movies is apparent. Comics are storyboards that never made it to the film studio—but they track the action just the same. Students who are making their own films can benefit from an analysis of the comic book format as they plan their shots and sequences. The connection of words and images can be investigated in comics: How do the pictures relate to the story? Which came first, the illustrations (as is sometimes the case with Marvel Comics) or the dialogue (the more usual approach)? How does the size and positioning of the panels on a page influence the way the story proceeds? And finally, students might be interested in producing their own comic, following, perhaps, the format of a favorite publication and telling a story—factual or fantasized—from their own experiences.

None of these activities requires great mental acumen, and yet they can all stretch the perception of students at many levels. They might even allow you, the teacher, to bypass the traditional duck into a phonebooth or uttering of a mystical word, and become, in the eyes of your students, a superhero nonetheless.

COMICS IN THE CLASSROOM

Neil Ellman

Once upon a time, children were warned not to play with matches, take candy from strangers, and read comic books. Educators were especially concerned about the latter, for they feared that comic books were so educationally unsound that their use would lead to mental stagnation and moral decay. While such fears may have been extreme, they were not entirely without basis, for the comic books of the 1940's and 1950's were as replete with scenes of cruelty and violence as they were with those of juvenile fatuousness.

Nevertheless, the content of comic books did change as a result of public and government pressure, and the increasing popularity of such reading made the phenomenon difficult for educators to ignore. The growth of television lent additional respectability to the concept of visual literacy and suggested to some educators that the era of print literacy was coming to an end. Television itself brought the comics to life as no other medium could.

At first, the educational value of comic books and strips was viewed largely as a matter of stimulation for unmotivated learners. The medium was used more in a diversionary than a substantive way. With time, however, comics became meaningful tools in the educational process and themselves became objects of study in courses on art, literature, and contemporary culture. Educators in almost every discipline have found ways to make use of the medium they once considered anathema.

James W. Brown (1977) provides a theoretical framework in which comics may be used in the foreign language classroom. The framework, which also has relevance for other academic areas, encompasses the linguistic and visual codes of which comics are made, and which should be taught to students as a means of deciphering the codes:

Linguistic Code

Primary Codes

1. The verbal narrative (if any) and its functions (e.g., to introduce characters and situations, to make commentaries, etc.).

Reprinted by permission of the author and the Association for Educational Communications and Technology from *Audiovisual Instruction* 24 (May 1979): 24-25.

2. The balloons (if any) and their functions (e.g., dialogue simulation, indirect communications with the reader).

Secondary Codes

1. Narrative: corresponds to formal and standard written discourse, and its sociocultural connotations.

2. Balloons: correspond to formal, informal, or substandard spoken discourse, and its sociocultural connotations.

Visual Code

Primary Codes

1. Layout of images on the page and their formal, sequential, or logical function in the narrative (e.g., their syntax).

2. Individual images: their size, position in the sequence, graphic characteristics, color.

Secondary Codes

1. Characterization: pictorial representation as an index of attitudes, states of mind, sociological background, etc.

2. Decor: setting as an index of economic status, class affiliation, local color, etc.

Brown goes on to cite the work of French scholars in developing innovative uses of comics to teach linguistics, culture, and literature. Linguistic exercises include: transcribing the written content in indirect style; orally reading the balloons with appropriate intonation; creating dialogue for blank balloons; and imagining the characters' thoughts. Culture can be studied through the analysis of the linguistic and visual codes, for both often indicate cultural differences. And literature can be emphasized, without assuming the intrinsic literary merit of comics, by studying the medium as a form of narrative and by comparing its structure and approach to those in other narrative forms.

A similar approach is taken by Robert J. Elkins and Christian Brüggemann (1971), whose specific concern is the teaching of English as a Second Language. They report that American comic strips and cartoons can be useful in ESL classes because such material introduces variety and provides an inside look into American life and thought. Many current popular comic strips have cultural, social and political significance and discuss the American way of life, society, and the individual.

Foreign and second language study, of course, have implications for the study of one's native language. Emma Halstead Swain (1978) provides an information matrix for designing comic book and strip activities in language arts and reading. On one axis, she identifies the grade and ability level to be taught; and on the other, the type of information available, based on her own survey, to design appropriate activities. For example, among the information listed next to "Junior high students who make poor grades," is the following information:

- Features that help students read comic books:
  Pictures
  Title
  Easy Words
  Action
  Characters

- What students like best about comic books:
  Characters
  Illustration
  Stories
  Announcements
  Letters to the editor

- Favorite comic book characters:
  Batman
  Charlie Brown
  Archie
  Spiderman
  Richie Rich

- Favorite comic strip characters:
  Dennis the Menace
  Charlie Brown
  Nancy
  Snoopy
  Blondie

In addition, Swain lists twenty suggestions for reading and language arts activities involving such areas as consonant blends, picture interpretation, possessives, special print, following directions, reading for details, summarization, detecting mood, predicting outcome, characterization, and alphabetical order. For the improvement of sensitivity to figurative language, students can be asked to find as many slang words as possible in a comic book and define the words using context clues. For the development of critical reading skills, students can be asked to list all the clues in a comic book that indicate that the story is not realistic.

Still another area in which comics are being used successfully is remediation of learning disabilities. Phyllis N. Hallenbeck (1976) states that comics are especially good for developing conceptual and logical abilities, such as sequencing, abstract thinking, and class inclusion. For the dyslexic child, they offer practice in left-to-right eye movement, discrimination of important details, and the general process of reading itself. Guided work with comics may help children to distinguish between fantasy and reality, as well as to express themselves verbally in a clearer manner. Best of all, Hallenbeck reports, the time spent in developing an understanding and appreciation for comics can benefit learning disabled children's comprehension of social situations, develop their sense of humor, and provide them with an enjoyable leisure time activity.

In these and other areas of the curriculum, comics have gained increased respectability. Teachers, it appears, have come a long way in their acceptance and use of popular materials. Charlie Brown may not be Othello, but if he can help students to learn to read, write, and think, neither is he the Big Bad Wolf.

References and Selected Bibliography

Arlin, Marshall and Garry Roth. "Pupils' Use of Time While Reading Comics and Books." *American Educational Research Journal*, V (Spring 1978), 201-16.

Brown, James W. "Comics in the Foreign Language Classroom: Pedagogical Perspectives." *Foreign Language Annals*, X (February 1977), 18-25.

Carillo, Bert B. "The Academic Uses of Mexican Comics." *Accent on ACTFL*, V (1975), 8-9.

Carlyle, Ann. "Comic Book Club." *Learning*, XI (April 1978), 48.

Elkins, Robert J. and Christian Brüggemann. "Comic Strips in the Teaching of English as a Foreign Language." Paper presented to a conference on the teaching of English, Kassel, West Germany, 1971. ED 056 591.

Gill, Robert et al. "The Effects of Cartoon Characters as Motivators of Pre-school Disadvantaged Children." OEO-8124, Final Report, 1970. ED 045 210.

Gomes de Matos, Francisco. "Djever Think About Comic Books? Creativity: New Ideas in Language Teaching," 1975. ED 105 769.

Hallenbeck, Phyllis N. "Remediating with Comic Strips." *Journal of Learning Disabilities*, IX (January 1976), 11-15.

Paine, Carolyn A. "Comics for Fun and Profit." *Learning*, III (October 1974), 86-89.

Swain, Emma Halstead. "Using Comic Books to Teach Reading and Language Arts." *Journal of Reading*, XXII (December 1978), 253-58.

I

WHERE?

- in any classroom for new teaching strategies

- in a junior high school library as the catalyst for increasing usage

- in social studies reporting

- in the science classroom for generating discussion

- in the political science classroom to illustrate lectures, stimulate discussions, and encourage students to think

- in an American history class for students to produce their own comic books

- in English instruction to motivate students to write

- in high school Latin courses for studying the classics

- in reading and language arts activities

THE FUNNIES AREN'T JUST FUNNY....
USING CARTOONS AND COMICS TO TEACH

June Rose Richie

Dr. Edward DeRoche, nationally known Newspaper in Education consultant from Marquette University, stated in a recent address that there are too many two-by-four teachers, too many who limit their teaching and the learning experiences of their students to the two covers of the textbook and the four walls of the classroom.[1] The newspaper is the resource and the tool that can broaden student experiences in learning and bring reality into the classroom. The newspaper is fresh and different every day and can indeed be labeled "a living textbook." One of the strongest points of rationale for using the newspaper is that it provides relevancy and it updates teaching. We know that most textbooks are outdated before they reach the classroom. There are many other plusses for using the newspaper. It helps the teacher individualize; contrary to what the teacher might have heard, the newspaper is written on a variety of reading levels. There will be some part of the newspaper that even the slowest and most reluctant readers will be able to master. The use of the newspaper lends itself to a variety of instructional modes. The newspaper is an economical curriculum material; most publishers sell their newspapers to schools for one-half the regular price, and a few give them to schools.

Using the newspaper allows a teacher to develop creativity, and a creative teacher fosters creativity in his/her students. Since the newspaper has an adult image, slow readers who may be able to work with comics only will not be ashamed to walk around with a newspaper under their arms as they might be a remedial reading text. The newspaper contains practical information about everyday working and living which is often not presented in textbooks. Reading and studying the newspaper under the guidance of a skilled teacher expands students' areas of interest, it expands their store of knowledge, and it opens up the world to them. Since most adults get much of their "post school" education from newspapers, it is important to teach students how to read a newspaper discriminately and to recognize the role of newspapers in society.

A resourceful teacher will utilize every part of a newspaper in his/her teaching—even the obituaries—but among the most versatile parts of the newspaper are the comics and cartoons. Most students are introduced to the newspaper on their parents' laps through the "funnies," so there is a built-in

Reprinted with permission of the author and Heldref Publications from *The Clearing House* (November 1979, vol. 53, no. 3): 125-28, a publication of the Helen Dwight Reid Educational Foundation.

motivation to learn through the comics. The comics are informal and consumable. They can be cut apart, drawn on, and colored with no fear of reprimand. This is certainly not true of textbooks. Comics are interesting; young people do not consider comics dull, because they are pictorial, colorful, and humorous. When comics are utilized in the classroom, students do not feel that the comics are being forced on them as they sometimes feel about a reading series. Comics show the world and life in a novel way by taking the serious and animating it. This may well be why children choose to read them. Comics can teach one in a lighthearted way how to deal successfully with the real world. For example, values clarification is often a major consideration in comics, especially in "Doonesbury" and "B.C." Cartoonist Morris Turner, creator of "Wee Pals," a cartoon strip which appears in *The San Diego Union*, and a film entitled "Kid Power" has dedicated his talent to enlighten young people on such topics as human rights, equal employment opportunity, and the role the basics play in any vocation. Comics are informative. From them the student can learn new vocabulary, the difference between antonyms and synonyms, configuration, sequence, sentence structure, different dialects, and punctuation.[2]

Before students begin working seriously with cartoons and comics, they need to learn more about the material they will be utilizing. Teachers can give valuable orientation through exercises which force the student to examine and analyze this new resource. Using the comics sections, students might supply true-false answers to such statements as the following:

- comics strip characters never seem to grow old;
- comic strips always use easy words;
- comic strips are only meant to make you laugh;
- all comic strips tell a continued story;
- comic strip people's words are always in a balloon;
- the comic strip story is told using only pictures and the characters' words;
- a comic strip always has four picture panels;
- all picture panels are the same width;
- comic strips show closeup and faraway shots;
- politics are not mentioned in comic strips.

Further analysis could be undertaken by asking students to find two examples of each of the following kinds of comics and supply the names and cartoonists for the strips:

- comics that are similar to human actions (realistic);
- comics that show a human weakness;

- comics aimed at boys and girls;
- comics aimed at adults;
- comics that may be helpful to society;
- comics that teach a lesson.

In addition to giving students background knowledge which would allow them to use the comics more effectively, these questions will stimulate interesting discussion.

With the advanced knowledge in learning psychology that we now have access to, educators realize that students are different and learn in different ways and at different rates. Much has been written about individualizing instruction and many efforts have been made to individualize. Despite efforts to individualize on a curriculum-wide basis through such techniques as modular scheduling, elective courses, and ability grouping, the most effective individualization takes place within the classroom. Comics and cartoons can be used to individualize instruction in a number of ways. Many teachers develop Learning Activity Packages (LAP's) to be used by individual students as remedial work or for enrichment. Two groups of teachers developed LAP's employing Wonderwoman and Snoopy themes to provide orientation to the newspaper. Another group of teachers developed a LAP to teach writing skills and used various cartoons and cartoon characters to make them interesting and colorful. Another LAP to teach the difference between fact and opinion utilized cartoon/comics to a great extent. When developing a LAP, one should be careful to state the objectives in terms that the student can understand, supply a variety of learning activities, and include measures by which the student can evaluate himself — by pre-testing, post-testing, and activity checks.

Perhaps more frequently developed than LAP's are folders to be used by individual students. These folders, which usually deal with a single skill or concept, are relatively inexpensive and easy to develop. The comics are a natural in developing folders. Most any language skill can be taught by utilizing the comics. Using one large "Family Circus" comic, one teacher asked the student to list ten adjectives and ten nouns. Another teacher, using the same comic, listed fifteen words and asked the student to supply a rhyming word for each. Still another teacher utilized this comic by listing fifteen words, first and last letters only, and asked the student to fill in the blank to learn to spell the words. Another teacher developed a folder by listing six words from a "Winky Ryatt" comic strip and asking the student to supply a synonym; and another teacher, using a "Peanuts" comic strip, listed twelve words and asked the student to supply a homonym for each. Using a "Shoe" strip, one teacher dealt with spelling, synonyms, and newspaper terms in a folder. Using "Dennis the Menace," one teacher asked the student to list four contractions used and to write the words for which each contraction had been substituted. One "Nancy" comic strip contained 18 misspelled words and was a natural for teaching spelling skills. Some students, even those on the secondary level, have difficulty with sequence. One teacher developed a folder in which the frames of a "Ziggy" strip had been cut apart and scrambled. The student was to indicate the correct order of the frames by numbering them. Another folder was developed by asking the student to find in a "Shoe" strip examples of the four kinds of sentences and then to generate a sentence based on the strip. Suffixes and prefixes can be taught through the comics. One teacher used a "Peanuts" strip to ask the students to list three words that ended in "ing" and to make three new words by adding "ing" to root words in the strip. In most instances, the answers should be somewhere in the folder—on the back, under a flap, or in a pocket—so the student may check himself. Both LAP's and folders should be laminated to preserve them and to allow for repeated use by students.

The use of comics/cartoons lends itself to the development of new teaching strategies. The cartoons/comics supply much good material for role playing, unrehearsed dramatization which often deals with a social or psychological problem. In role playing, there is no rehearsing, no memorizing of lines, no coaching; its value as a teaching device lies in its spontaneity and the individual's creative use of his own experience. An editorial cartoon which deals with some social or political problem might be interpreted by students through role playing. Such comic strips as "The Family Circus," "Dennis the Menace," and "Winky Ryatt," which deal with family situations, lend themselves readily to role playing. Role playing comics/cartoons may serve as a springboard to the study of some selection in the anthology or may lead to the study of a thematic unit.

The use of comics/cartoons lends itself well to small group work, where students have an opportunity to exchange ideas, pool their resources, and develop cooperative work habits. Working with a section of comics, one group might take a "Ziggy" strip which has no dialogue and write dialogue for it. In this exercise, they would be developing their skills of interpretation as well as writing and punctuation skills. Another group might take a strip such as "Winky Ryatt," which often depicts teenage situations, and develop a skit based on the situation presented. Another group might take a strip such as "Doonesbury" and discuss the use of satire by cartoonist Trudeau. Another group using a "Blondie" strip, which often presents some marital problem, might exercise their creative writing skills by writing a sequel or a conclusion to a particular strip. Another group, using strips such as "Rex Morgan" or "Judge Parker" which often present social problems, might be stimulated to conduct research and present a report on some social or political problem. Further analysis of the comics can be made by asking small groups of students to find comics which illustrate the following:

- economic opportunity, i.e., opportunity for individuals to improve themselves by their own effort;
- wide participation in politics;
- belief in reform rather than revolution;
- a mobile population;
- high position and freedom for women;

- toleration of differences, i.e., freedom of worship, speech, assembly;

- world-wide responsibility;

- respect for the rights and abilities of the individual.

Games and puzzles which facilitate learning in a fun fashion can be developed easily with comics/cartoons. One teacher developed a game board to teach vowel sounds. Directions were given by comics characters' dialogue in balloons. Since this game is usually played by two to four students, they can check each other. This same teacher developed a second game board featuring directions given by comics characters to further refine skills in using short and long vowels. One teacher developed a board which can be adapted to teaching any skill by writing different directions in the laminated balloons. A grid puzzle which contained the names of nineteen comic strip characters going horizontally, vertically, or diagonally was developed by one teacher. Another teacher developed a crossword puzzle containing thirteen names or terms relating to comic strips. These puzzles presented opportunities for students to sharpen their spelling, vocabulary, and locational skills.

The comics and cartoons can be utilized to teach values clarification. One of the most effective activities is to ask each student to design from a piece of poster board his/her own coat-of-arms, decorating it any way he/she chooses. The student divides the coat-of-arms into six sections and illustrates the statement in each section with a picture or word from the comics. The six statements are as follows:

(1) One thing that I am very good at and one thing that I want to be better at;

(2) My most important material possession;

(3) What I would do with my life if I had only one year to do whatever I wanted and would be guaranteed success;

(4) One thing I believe in and would never change my mind about;

(5) My greatest achievement of the past year and my greatest failure of the past year;

(6) Three things people would say about me if my life ended today.

This activity allows for deep introspection on the part of the student and gives the teacher insight into what "makes the student tick." Students are usually eager to explain their selections to the class and to have their work displayed in the classroom.

Career education can be taught through utilizing cartoons/comics. Teachers and students can collect cartoons and comics which reflect attitudes about work and careers. These can be used to stimulate discussions on careers and the work ethic. The teacher can ask the students to search a comics section to see how many jobs or occupations are represented in the comics. This might arouse curiosity about qualifications, duties, and remuneration for certain jobs.

Critical thinking can be taught through the skillful use of an editorial cartoon and a corresponding editorial. The point should be made that the featured editorial cartoon does not always correspond to or relate to the editorial of the day but often does. The study might begin by discussing the symbols used in the editorial cartoon. Symbolism is often a hard concept for students to grasp. From the cartoon, the discussion might move to the editorial. The teacher could lead the class in a discussion of the purpose of the editorial and help students distinguish between statements of fact and statements of opinion found in the editorial.

There is no limit to the number of concepts and skills in reading, writing, thinking, and literary terminology that an imaginative teacher can present through comics and cartoons. The important thing is that teachers are developing their creativity and students are lifted out of the deadly doldrums of drill and are having fun while they learn.

Notes

[1]Edward F. DeRoche, Speech Presented at the Newspaper in the Classroom Workshop, Memphis State University, Memphis, Tennessee, August 7, 1978.

[2]Copley Newspapers Educational Services *NIE Teacher's Exchange*, 1:2 (February 1978), p. 1.

SPIDER-MAN AT THE LIBRARY   Larry Dorrell and Ed Carroll

SPIDER-MAN and his friends have found a home in the West Junior High School library in Columbia, Missouri. Comic books in the school library? Comic books infiltrated public schools years ago and have long been a source of conflict between teachers and students. Can comic books, a medium that many educators believe is an antithetical to the basic idea of education, be seriously considered by school librarians?

As a result of the experiences with comic books in the West Junior High School library, the answer to that question is most certainly in the affirmative.

During the summer of 1979, a decision was made to work on improving the school library's image. It was underused because of some students' negative feelings about the library. They did not feel welcome in the library and thought it had nothing to offer them. In an attempt to overcome these perceptions, the library offered comic books to students during the 1979-1980 school year.

Why use comic books to improve the library's image? Comic books are a part of the junior-high-age students' world. Comic-book heroes are a part of our video culture. The Batman series of the 1960s was just the first of many such programs for television. Now Stan Lee's Marvel Comics Group and the D.C. Comics Group are well represented on Saturday morning television. "The Incredible Hulk," along with "Wonder Woman," "Spider-Man," "Captain America," and others became an important part of television viewing by junior-high-age students. Comic-book heroes are increasingly more visible.

It was thought that if the students' interest in leisure-time activities could be used to create an interest in their school library, an important and valuable ally would be available for education. So comic books were added to the library to determine if they would prove to be an ally for education.

The introduction of comic books presented two questions: Would they motivate students to use the school library? And, Would increased library traffic result in increased noncomic book circulation? To answer these questions, data on library traffic and circulation at West Junior High School were collected from October 15, 1979 to May 7, 1980 (see chart). Since the major concern was in the development of both potential and actual library users, the number of students who came to the library (potential users) and the statistics of noncomic book circulation (actual users) served as the dependent variables. To serve as a base for comparison, data were collected for the control group from October 15, 1979 to

Reprinted with permission of the authors and the publisher from *School Library Journal* 27 (August 1981): 17-19. R. R. Bowker Co./A Xerox Corporation.

January 16, 1980. Data were collected for the treatment group from January 17, 1980 to May 7, 1980.

During both the control and treatment periods, adjusted traffic counts were determined by a count of all students who entered the library during regular hours. Students who were brought to the library by their teachers to work on class assignments were not counted in the adjusted traffic figure.

During the control period, 15,539 students were counted as adjusted traffic. That number was divided by the 57 days of the control period to obtain a daily average of 272.61 students. During the treatment period, 36,732 students were counted, and that number was divided by the 74 days of the period to give a daily average of 496.38. To obtain the percentage of increase, we divided the treatment daily average by the control daily average. The resulting figure indicated that there was an 82 percent increase in adjusted traffic.

LIBRARY TRAFFIC & CIRCULATION

PRE COMIC CONTROL
10/15/79-1/16/80

	Adjusted Traffic	Circu-lation
Control period (57 days) totals	15,539	4,417
Control period daily average	272.61	77.49

COMIC BOOK TREATMENT
1/17/80-5/7/80

	Adjusted Traffic	Circu-lation
Treatment period (74 days) totals	36,732	7,473
Treatment period daily average	496.38	100.99
Percentage of change	+ .82	+ .30

Library traffic experienced an immediate and lasting change after the introduction of comic books into the school library. It was not until the end of the school year that daily traffic began to decrease. Much of that decrease was a result of the normal decrease in the use of the library during the last few days of the school year. Not once during the treatment period did a daily count drop below the highest daily count of the control period.

During the treatment period, circulation of noncomic book materials increased by 30 percent over the control period. Circulation counts were determined by an end-of-the-day count of items checked out by students. The counts did not include any circulation by the faculty nor did it include items used by the students in the library or for daily use in their classrooms. Comic books were not circulated and, therefore, were not included in the circulation counts.

During the control period, 4,417 items were circulated. That number was divided by the 57 days of the control period to obtain a daily average of 77.49 items. During the treatment period, 7,473 items were counted, and that number was divided by the 74 days of the period to give a daily average of 100.99. To obtain the percentage of increase, the treatment daily average was divided by the control daily average. The resulting figure indicated a 30 percent increase in circulation.

Throughout the treatment period, the circulation ranged from a low of 76.6 during the last five days of counting in May 1980, to a high of 119.44 in March 1980.

Circulation, like traffic, obtained its greatest increase about midway in the treatment period. In March, the average daily circulation had increased by 54 percent over the average of the control period.

There is some indication that the impact of comic books on circulation was not as immediate as the impact on traffic. The only times circulation dropped below the daily average, for the control period, was during the first two weeks and the last five days of the treatment period. The greatest percentage of decrease for any month during the treatment period, when compared to the daily average of 77.49 of the control period, was a little over 1 percent during May. The overall increase in circulation of 30 percent was a substantial increase in circulation over the control period. This is just as exciting and rewarding as a 30 percent increase in grade averages is to classroom teachers.

No advance notice was given when the comic books were introduced into the library. When students arrived during the first period of school on Thursday, January 17, 1980, they found the comic books displayed on a rack in the library's periodical section. But no student read a comic book during the first two periods. In fact, when the students did notice the comic books, they simply ignored their presence. Apparently students were suffering from the same ideas as many educators: Comic books are not educational; they are "forbidden fruit" that are not read openly in school and should be avoided. In the third period, when the librarian spent time moving and regrouping the comic books, the first few students gradually began to venture over. Once the ice was broken by these students, word spread throughout the school. By the fifth period, the students were coming to the library and going directly to the comic book rack.

Security

At the end of the first day, a count was made, and 10 percent of the comic books were missing. But after a while, the loss stopped, and the missing comic books began to reappear. And, in the last month of the school year, the collection actually grew by 8 percent when students brought in their old comic books and added them to the library's collection.

The initial loss might have been avoided if the students had been prepared for the comic books and had been told, in advance, that comic books did not circulate. Another possible solution to the problem would have been to allow students to check them out since the staff received a large number of requests to borrow the comic books.

The next school year, the comic books were displayed in locking periodical holders and not one comic book has been lost since.

Observations

The change in library usage at West Junior High School may not be completely due to the comic books, but they did serve as the catalyst for increased usage. Comic books signaled students that there was something in the library for them; that the library was open and comfortable. This overall perception of comic books as an indication of an open climate may have contributed greatly to the increase in both library traffic and circulation.

Comic books in the library were associated with improvement in student behavior within the school library. The number of students who were returned to study centers because they were unable to act appropriately in the library decreased greatly after comic books were introduced. Students who had been discipline problems changed their behavior. The library staff and teachers of some of the special students used comics to encourage better behavior in the library and in the classroom. Those students were told that they would not be given library passes if they did not behave properly in the classroom. The teachers and the library staff are convinced that this worked because these students really wanted to read the comic books.

As far as the reception by parents, the comic books did not produce any negative responses from the school district's patrons—not a single negative complaint was received. In fact, a number of positive statements were received by the school administrators and the library staff. The teachers (especially the reading and special ed teachers) supported the idea of making comic books available in the library and lent their encouragement.

Building a Collection

It is recommended that school librarians who decide to provide comic books to students not attempt to buy a large number of titles. A collection of 40 to 50 titles, selected according to the reading interest of the students and replaced, each month, with the latest editions, should be sufficient for a junior high school of less than 1000 students. West Junior High School's experience with comic books indicated that the numbers of noncirculating comic books should be kept to a manageable size. Circulation policies on comic books should be similar to the policies of other periodicals, with provisions for a limited circulation of the current issue and more liberal circulation of back issues.

Comic books present a greater security problem for the library than regular books, but the use of locking periodical holders eliminated this problem at West Junior High School. Comic books are still inexpensive; the library administration might simply want to consider those comic books that are missing as expendable items. Comic books have proven to be a good, inexpensive investment for the library, which is currently purchasing 40 individual titles from Marvel, D.C. and Archie Comics at a total cost of less than $20 a month. The 40 locking periodical holders were obtained for $200. This is a one-time investment that will be used for years and thus is not a great cost. Many school districts spend far greater amounts attempting to foster students' interest in using the school library.

It is the responsibility of the school librarians and the school administration to make the school library an important part of the school. Library traffic and circulation both indicate how students use the library.

Spider-Man and his friends have provided the library with unexpected and welcome changes in student attitudes towards their library. This is reflected in the great increase in the numbers of students who use their library and the number of items which circulate.

If Spider-Man and his friends can provide your library with greater appeal to students, then is it not time to turn to comics? You too may be able to use comics to rescue your library and restore its appeal to students. Can Spider-Man save your school library?

REPORT MAKING—
THE CARTOON WAY

Frank W. Sosnowski

Before I introduce my students to the traditional social studies research report, they work on a cartoon report. All the important information is included, plus illustrations within a series of several cartoon blocks.

This kind of report has several advantages: (1) It means the student must visualize what he or she is writing about. (2) The student has to study maps, pictures and graphs in the source material in addition to the text. (3) Because students must limit their explanations to fit the cartoon frames, they tend to be more concise. They learn to rely more on effective illustrations to present information. (4) The final cartoon research reports are colorful and interesting for display.

Students who might normally resist reading a traditionally written report will look carefully at a cartoon report. The children learn by studying one another's reports.

Getting Ready

Before I assign the cartoon research reports, I make sure my students have learned or reviewed how to use the dictionary and book indices and practiced these research skills. They also know that it is important to use more than one book in gathering information and that there are many possible sources.

Our first reports are on countries. Through class discussion, I have my students develop a set of questions that pertain to any country. I write these on the chalkboard, grouping them logically when possible.

These questions are important because they provide the students with some guidance in their research. When they read with specific questions in mind, they get more from their reading and remember more.

When the questions are decided on, I copy, duplicate and distribute them. Be sure your students understand that they are not expected to answer all the questions nor should they feel limited by these questions. Encourage them to include other information that may be particularly appropriate to their country.

Reprinted from *Teacher* 92 (March 1975): 75-77. Copyright © 1975 by Macmillan Professional Magazines. Used by permission of The Instructor Publications, Inc.

The lists compiled by classes can vary greatly in the number of questions. For younger children, you may want to keep the list short and simple. One of my sixth-grade classes drew up this long list:

1. Where is the country located?
   - [ ] What countries neighbor it?
   - [ ] What bodies of water border it?
   - [ ] What is its latitudinal and longitudinal location?
   - [ ] What continent is it on?
   - [ ] What hemisphere is it in?

2. What is its climate?

3. What are its major mountain ranges?

4. What kind of vegetation does it have?
   - [ ] Is it sparsely or densely populated?
   - [ ] What is the population per square mile?

6. What does the flag look like?

7. What are the national physical characteristics of its people?

8. What are the country's most important tourist attractions?

9. What are the major natural resources?

10. What kind of homes do the people live in?

11. What form of government does it have?

12. What are the major languages?

13. What are the main products?

14. What kind of food crops are raised?

15 What animals are raised?

16. What are the major physical regions of the country?

17. What is the national dress?

18. What are the major means of communication?

19. What are the common means of transportation?

20. What are the common forms of entertainment?
    - [ ] What are the favorite sports?
    - [ ] What are the major holidays?

21. Are there any unique customs?

22. What is the fauna (natural animal life)?

23. What are the major exports?

24. What are the major imports?

25. What are the chief characteristics of the art?

26. What are the chief power sources?

27. What are the common occupations?

28. What special food or delicacies are eaten?

29. What is the capital?

30. What are the major cities?

31. What is the currency?

32. What is the average income?

33. What is the educational system like?

34. What size is the country?

35. What does its name mean?

36. Who are its rulers?

37. In what major wars has it participated?

38. When was the country first established or formed?

39. Who are some native historical figures?
    - ☐ Artists?
    - ☐ Rulers?
    - ☐ Musicians?

Making the Report

After our list of questions is compiled, duplicated and distributed, the students are given large sheets of paper. The size varies from year to year, depending on what is available. One inexpensive source is paper that has been used only on one side and that you can obtain from local business firms. I explain to the children that they will divide the paper into various sized cartoon frames based on what information they decide to present in them.

I encourage my students to use their textbooks as the first source of information. Additional source materials are library books, encyclopedias and available periodicals. An almanac will often provide the most current statistical information.

After making notes that answer some of the questions on the class list or some of their own, the students decide which facts they want to present in how many cartoon frames and how these will be illustrated. Then, in pencil, they draw the frames and illustrations and print the explanatory material.

After I've met with each student and each one has checked his or her spelling, grammar and so on, they are ready to finish the reports. First they print over the penciled letters with a felt-tip or ink pen, erasing all pencil markings. Pictures are colored with crayon, felt-tip pens or pencil crayons.

When the reports are completed, they are displayed in the school hallway where they can be read at leisure by students in the class and by other students in the school. Some of the cartoon reports are selected for general display in our public library.

Doing cartoon research reports can serve as an effective stepping-stone toward writing the traditional report. Students are particularly pleased with their results.

CARTOON SCHOOLING

David C. Ulmer, Jr.

"Once upon a time in the land of the free, there were folks who had lots of the good things of life." Thus begins a "fairy tale come true" about energy and environment which I have written and illustrated with editorial cartoons, clipped from newspapers over the years.

The story, projected on an overhead projector, has proved enormously successful in my science classroom for generating discussion in areas where science and social science cross paths.

My story, which I titled "Thrice Upon a Time: A Story About Then and Now as It Applies to Maybe," uses 24 cartoons to trace America's energy story—from "the good old days" through today's inertia in coping with the energy problem. It concludes with one of my favorite cartoons—that of an extraterrestrial "visitor" standing on the steps of Congress and reporting home his conclusion, "Earth shows no sign of intelligent life."

There are other ways cartoons might be used. One might provide students with copies of selected editorial cartoons and ask them to compose their own stories—or even their own cartoons.

Reprinted with the permission of the author and the publisher from *Science Teacher* 45 (May 1978): 44.

THE POLITICAL CARTOON AS A TEACHING DEVICE

William Ray Heitzmann

The diversity of the political cartoon lends itself to utilization by instructors to educate and motivate their students. The cartoon, an imprecise term, is basically an interpretive picture which makes use of symbolism and, most often, bold and humorous exaggeration to present a message or point of view concerning people, events, or situations. It conveys its message quickly—sometimes subtly, sometimes brashly—but generally gets its point across to more people than do editorials (Weaver, 1965).

The cartoon has natural appeal to students, and it serves as an excellent springboard for discussions. Not only can cartoons promote classroom interaction and enable the instructor to involve reticent students but, properly utilized, they can encourage students to operate at higher cognitive levels (Heitzmann, 1974).

Similarly, this art form nicely illustrates lectures and permits faculty to add not only pizazz but also humor to the learning process; the value of comic relief has long been recognized in the classroom. As cartoons vary in sophistication, the teacher can use appropriate ones to assess the learners' knowledge of the subject matter (Bennett and Heitzmann, 1975).

Scott Long, award-winning cartoonist for the *Minneapolis Tribune*, explains the power of his art form:

> A political cartoon can be an awesome weapon, even poisonous, some would say. It can floor an argument with a single devastating blow ... a cartoon can break the language barrier and convey a common meaning to all men everywhere. It can anger us, it can make us laugh, it can make us weep. It thrives on crisis and must be used with caution [Brooks, 1973].

Guidance in selecting cartoons comes from Nevins and Weitenkampf (1944), who discuss three requirements of a "really good cartoon." The first, "wit or humor," is usually obtained by exaggeration; it should be slick and not merely done for comic effect. Surely most contemporary cartoons meet this criterion, as do the classics of Nast, Keppler, and others. Secondly, it must have a basis in truth, and the characters, though embodying philosophical biases, must have

Reprinted with permission of the author and Heldref Publications from *Teaching Political Science* 6 (January 1979): 166-84, a publication of the Helen Dwight Reid Educational Foundation.

"recognizability" to the viewer. The importance of the identification of one's caricatures plagues every artist. Whereas Nast's Tweed, McCutcheon's Teddy Roosevelt, and Levine's LBJ are instantly recognizable, Herblock's Ford may take longer for the viewer to associate the reality with the illustration. Herblock's Nixon met this criterion so well that the former president reputedly remarked prior to the 1960 election campaign, "I have to erase the Herblock image" (Potter, 1959).

Hesse, in 1959, observed that in recent years (post World War II) key political figures almost exclusively provided the basis for the caricature. This trend has continued.

Moral purpose exists as the third requirement; "without moral earnestness, no cartoonist is likely to give his work a quality of universality or permanence." This attribute has memorialized the works of great cartoonists.

Political science instructors are fortunate in that, though a young country, America has a rich cartoon heritage.

America's Political Cartoon Heritage: The First Century

Whereas many contemporary cartoonists such as Herblock, Manning, Mauldin, and Oliphant have a style and audience of their own (many of the prominent cartoonists are syndicated and appear in numerous newspapers), their early American counterparts were strongly influenced by British cartoons and did not enjoy either the recognition or the financial rewards of today's artists. Early illustrations were generally crowded with figures, overdrawn, and viciously satirical; dialogue was frequently lengthy and illegible. Ben Franklin's "Join or Die" (severed snake) remains a notable exception. Franklin's cartoon, the first to appear in an American newspaper (*The Pennsylvania Gazette*, May 9, 1754), drawn to stimulate support for the Albany Plan of Union, appeared in every American newspaper shortly after its initial publication. The snake, which he drew divided into eight parts, had been chosen because of a popular superstition of the time that a severed serpent had the ability to reunite and come back to life. During the Stamp Act Crisis (1765) and the beginning of the Revolution (1774), it again appeared and received wide circulation (Culhane, 1975). This cartoon can be worked nicely into discussions of federalism and expansion of the national government.

Most of the early cartoons, like present-day newspaper articles, lacked a signature; consequently they frequently remain anonymous. This anonymity of the cartoonist, and absence of libel laws, frequently resulted in biting satire (Becker, 1959). The inability of newspapers to pay cartoonists and the costliness of reproducing the woodcuts and copper engravings upon which the artist worked in a large part accounted for the paucity of cartoons during the Colonial era and the early years of the Republic (Hess and Kaplan, 1968). Some cartoons did gain exposure as posters during this period. One classic that appeared in the early years was Elkanah Tisdale's "Gerrymander" (1812). This cartoon, produced as a critique of the newly created Essex senatorial district, took the shape of a winged vulture; the Massachusetts Governor Elbridge Gerry lent his name to the title. As a result, a new word was added to the language. Teachers investigating redistricting and "one man-one vote" may wish to utilize this drawing.

While the exact origin of the symbol for the United States—Uncle Sam—remains uncertain, most historians trace it to this period. One Samuel Wilson, nicknamed "Uncle Sam," of Troy, New York, supplied meat and other goods to the military during the War of 1812; he stenciled "U.S." on his products; eventually it became applied to the government as a whole. There exist several schools of thought on the basis for the traditional chinwhiskered "Uncle Sam" figure (Hess and Kaplan, 1968). Some argue that it is a caricature of Samuel Wilson who also provided the name "Uncle Sam"; others suggest it was an evolution of Brother Jonathan, who had earlier represented the United States (Nevins and Weitenkampf, 1944). Some believe "Uncle Sam" to be a product of a later period stereotyping the conservative American farmer of the late nineteenth century. Faculty who make the decision to integrate cartoons into their teaching should spend some time in explanation of the function of symbolism. Uncle Sam, the Democrat's donkey, and the Republican's elephant serve as excellent beginning points.

Just as the War of 1812 saw a growth of editorial cartoons, the development of lithography and the election campaign of 1828 stimulated a rapid expansion in the late 1820s. Lithography provided an inexpensive method of reproducing the cartoon, and the 1828 presidential contest produced controversial issues for the cartoonists; the victor, Andrew Jackson, provided additional material. Currier and Ives turned out some political lithographs—frequently taking both sides of an issue. However, politics was a relatively minor interest—out of an estimated 10 million copies only eighty were political illustrations (Hess and Kaplan, 1968).

Cartooning expanded not only in circulated lithographic prints but in the newspapers. This latter development was stimulated by an expansion of the newsprint publishing industry. The *New York Herald* and the *New York Tribune*, led respectively by James Gordon Bennett and Horace Greeley, contributed to the use and popularity of the cartoon. Political illustrations rarely appeared in magazines at this time, although some did. It remained for *Harper's Weekly* to be founded [1857] before America had a rival to such European greats as London's *Punch* and France's *Le Charivari!* Despite the growth of the art, cartoonists were still quite rare prior to the Civil War.

The appearance of Abraham Lincoln on the national scene and the commencing of the Civil War provided ample material for cartoonists. In his introduction to Wilson's (1953) *Lincoln in Caricature*, R. G. McMurtry observed, "Abraham Lincoln's homely features lend themselves to pictorial exaggeration; his long angular figure makes him the delight of cartoonists." The majority of Northern cartoonists showed themselves to be overwhelmingly sympathetic to the sixteenth president and the Union cause. A rare Southern cartoon appearing in one of the few outlets for political humor (*Southern Illustrated News, Southern Punch*, and *The Bugle Horn of Liberty*) might score a lucky hit on the president. However, it remained for the British cartoonists to fire the barbs at the "rail splitter." Matt Morgan, in *London Fun*, and John Tinnel, in *Punch*, for the major portion of the war, consistently and cynically worked their art; late in the war and particularly following the assassination, they changed from a position of criticism to one of support and finally reverence (Wilson, 1953). During the war a young cartoonist came to the aid of the Union and of the president; at the time Lincoln called him "our best recruiting sergeant." Historians have credited this young artist with strongly aiding Lincoln's election in 1864. His fame has been generally connected with his later successes; however, early efforts influenced the events of the 1860s; his name, Thomas Nast (Keller, 1968).

America's Cartoon Heritage:
The Second Century

The technique, influence, and success of Thomas Nast's work mark a turning point in America's political cartoon tradition and label him as the nation's first modern political cartoonist.

The German-born former battlefield illustrator first gained prominence with a biting indictment of northern appeasers in 1864 entitled "Compromise with the South." The illustration showed a defiant Confederate officer shaking hands with a crippled northern soldier over the grave of Union heroes. A black family shown in the background is again in chains; Columbia is kneeling crying over the grave. The Democrats had met a few days earlier in Chicago to nominate a presidential candidate and adopt a peace at any price platform; Nast believed this to be not compromise but surrender. Nast had joined the staff of *Harper's Weekly* two years earlier. Now it had become a political power. A major circulation builder, Nast helped the publication triple its readership during his fight with Tweed.

Nast's fame and his place in history largely rest upon his success in destroying the Tammany Ring and its head, "Boss" Tweed; the "Boss," a man of "rather commanding presence, who carried almost 300 pounds on a frame just short of six feet," reputedly offered the artist $100,000 to study art in Europe in order to stop "them damn pictures!" "The Brains," "Under the Thumb," "Who Stole the People's Money? — Do Tell, T'was Him," "A Group of Vultures Waiting for the Storm to 'Blow Over' — Let's Prey," "The Tammany Tiger Loose — What Are We Going to Do about It?," and "Something That Did Blow Over — November 7, 1871" (all drawn in 1871) are just a few of those that have come to be regarded as classic attacks upon corrupt urban political machines (Vinson, 1967).

Throughout his career, Nast generally strongly supported the Republican party; he remained steadfastly loyal to President Grant despite revelations of administrative corruption and mismanagement. In 1884, however, he defected to support the reformist Cleveland over the "plumed knight" James G. Blaine. Generally reformist in his views, Nast's deep anti-Catholicism and consequent anti-papal cartoons contrasted with his support of Orientals and blacks make him somewhat of an enigma. While some of his views may have been suspect, his fertile imagination was not; his use of the Democratic donkey, the Tammany tiger, and Republican elephant contributes to his reputation as America's premier cartoonist. As one who influenced presidential elections from 1864 to 1884 and of whom Grant stated, "He did as much as any man to preserve the Union," and as the nemesis of Tammany, he can justly be described as America's most influential cartoonist.[1] No course in urban politics or local government would be complete without an examination of Nast's work.

The years prior to the turn of the century, characterized by the entrance of Joseph Pulitzer and William Randolph Hearst into the newspaper industry, saw a rapid expansion of newspapers; it was this medium that would serve the cartoonists for the next three-quarters of a century. Every large daily newspaper featured a cartoon by 1900.

As has been seen, cartoonists, like journalists, need an issue or a personality for content; the Spanish-American War and the administration of President Roosevelt provided both. Spain quickly became the object for Pughe ("She is Getting Too Feeble to Hold Them," 1896) and Keppler ("Time Nearly Up," 1897); TR became a natural for caricature. The active, aggressive, trustbusting, sports-minded presdient was, in the words of cartoonist John T. McCutcheon, "an inexhaustible Golconda of inspiration for the cartoonist" (McCutcheon, 1909).

The outbreak of the world war in 1914 saw the birth of a steady flow of anti-German cartoons. New Yorkers included Nelson Harding (*Brooklyn Daily Eagle*), Robert Carter (*Evening World*), and Rollin Kirby (*World*). By 1918, a Bureau of Cartoons, established to suggest topics to cartoonists that would aid the war effort, was sending out a weekly bulletin. Not all cartoonists supported the growing militarism. Robert Minor, in the *Masses*, a Socialist magazine, published "Army Medical Examiner: 'At Last a Perfect Soldier!' " (1915), one of the most aggressive antiwar cartoons ever published, depicting a magnificent, physically conditioned body with no head (Becker, 1959).[2]

Cartooning in the postwar era mirrored the nation's concern with domestic as opposed to international affairs. While there was some concern with the League of Nations, Prohibition and its effects also occupied the illustrators. Rollin Kirby, winner of three Pulitzer prizes, concentrated several of his noteworthy efforts on the League: "The Accuser" (1920), "Triumphal Entry into Normalcy" (1920), and his 1925 Pulitzer Prize-winning "News from the Outside World." Kirby had won the first prize awarded in 1922 for "On the Road to Moscow"; in 1929 he won his third. The prize, awarded from the endowment of Joseph Pulitzer, has been handled through Columbia University (Becker, 1959). Kirby's impact was felt domestically also. In fact, his "Mr. Dry" came to symbolize the prohibition of liquor.

As the nation felt itself in the throes of the Great Depression, the dry days of Prohibition were quickly forgotten (and Prohibition, more quickly repealed). The 1932 Pulitzer Prize reflected this concern when the award went to John McCutcheon for his "A Wise Economist Asks a Question." The drawing features a squirrel asking "But Why Didn't You Save Some Money for the Future When Times Were Good?" The man, sitting on the park bench with a note titled "Victim of Back Failure" lying on his jacket, answers "I Did."

The rise of fascism abroad and FDR at home began to occupy the thoughts of the cartoon artists. The prize winners beginning in 1937 reflected the growing concern with the widening war. Charles D. Batchelor's "Come On In, I'll Treat You Right, I Used to Know Your Daddy" (1937), showed a prostitute labeled "War" during a European youth, proved prophetic. The trend continued—in 1938 with Vaughn Shoemaker's "The Road Back" (Hohenberg, 1959).

Faculty involved with international relations courses undoubtedly have recognized several opportunities for implementing cartoons in their classrooms; others follow.

Although not the object of cartoonists that his fifth cousin Teddy had been, FDR, four-time president and New Deal designer, provided content for several years but did not monopolize cartoonists as might have been expected. Not only did international issues provide FDR competition for editorial page sketches, but John Llewellyn Lewis, president of the United Mine Workers and founder of the Congress of Industrial Organizations, because of physical appearance, personality, and political clout, did the same. As one cartoonist explained, "John Llewellyn Lewis was without doubt one of God's greatest gifts to cartoonists in the twentieth century."

The Cold War era has had many issues to supply the artist. Rube Goldberg, who has lent his name to enlarging the vocabulary of Americans and who captured the 1948 Pulitzer award, typifies the beginning of Cold War cartoonists; his "Peace Today" shows an atom bomb precariously balanced between world control and world destruction. Except for the activity of some outstanding, widely circulated cartoonists (Conrad, Fischetti, Herblock, Long, Manning, Mauldin), the art during the 1950s seemed to enter a period of dormancy. British cartoonist Michael Cummings (Jones, 1971) makes this point while providing some insight into the profession:

> The first and major daily problem that far transcends the relatively simple task of drawing is finding the right idea. The cartoonist wakes in the morning and hopes a cartoon-worthy event has happened. If it has, he must digest the happening and form an opinion about it. He must then visualize it into an amusing picture which shows the paradoxical or sardonic aspect—with or without caption, he allows himself much artistic license, which is another way of describing caricature.

The quiet after the storm (World War II) produced few major issues or national personalities for cartoonists. The end of the tranquility of the 1950s and early 1960s marked the beginning of a new renaissance.

The Contemporary Scene

Beginning in the late sixties there was a reawakening in political illustrations. The expansion of the war in Vietnam, the protest movement, the criticism of

President Johnson, and the reappearance on the national scene of Richard Nixon first as candidate and then as president provided content for the cartoonists.

Unfortunately, in the recent newspaper market the novice fights an uphill battle because of a decline in the number of newspapers and the expansion of the syndication of many of the popular national cartoonists. Despite this trend, John Chase, political cartoonist for WDSV-TV in New Orleans, feels, "The American cartoonist in the 1960's has a considerable following in his own neighborhood, and his first responsibility is to be routinely effective and provocative to this regional readership" (Hess and Kaplan, 1968; Smith, 1954; Hesse, 1959). Chase has set a criterion for the local cartoonists—if unable to obtain a regional following, they will be replaced by a syndication.

Bill Mauldin, who gained fame with his World War II cartoons, returned to his profession in the late 1950s. During the early 1960s as the civil rights movement gained prominence, Mauldin produced several supportive cartoons. His "See You in Church" (1962) depicts two shady "klansmen-type" of persons carrying explosives, the implication being that, for some, racism and churchgoing are compatible. In the same vein, he drew an American eagle climbing a flagpole and telling the present sitter, "Jim Crow—I've decided I want my seat back" (1963; Hess and Kaplan, 1968). While some were aiming their barbs at southern rednecks, Jules Feiffer used the urban and suburban middle class for his targets. Feiffer, whose career began with the *Village Voice*, skillfully pointed out contradictions in the philosophy and practice of northern white liberals.

The caricature of LBJ became dominant during the middle 1960s; Paul Szep's (*Boston Globe*) characterization of LBJ as king in his "A Senator Fulbright to See You, Sire, Seems He Can Reconcile Himself to Your Infallibility" (1967) typifies the era (Hess and Kaplan, 1968). Szep's "The Summer of '73," depicting a gasoline truck out of gas with the driver walking to the nearest gas station, garnered the 1974 Pulitzer Prize (Brooks, 1975). Paul Conrad, *Los Angeles Times*, began his illustrations in 1950 with the *Denver Post* and gained national attention for his cartooning during the 1960s; presently, he is regarded as one of the nation's premier cartoonists. A Pulitzer Prize (1964, 1971) and Sigma Delta Chi Award (1970) winner, Conrad, like many of his fellow professionals, has focused most of his recent drawings on the Nixon presidency. Typical of this vintage is his "Man on a White Horse" (1974) showing the president attempting to mount a white horse by using booster boxes labeled "Personal Police Force," "IRS," "CIA," "Pentagon," and "FBI" (Brooks, 1975; Culhane, 1975). When Conrad moved from the *Post* to the *Times*, Pat Oliphant, recruited from Australia, took his place. Oliphant quickly responded to his new assignment, winning the Pulitzer Prize two years after his appointment. The cartoon "They Won't Get Us the Peace Table" (1966) shows Ho Chi Minh holding a dying Vietnamese in his arms (Culhane, 1975).

Herbert L. Block (Herblock), one of the most widely known and distinguished cartoonists, has earned many awards for cartooning: 1942 and 1954 Pulitzer prizes, 1951 Sigma Delta Chi Award, 1940 National Headliners Club Award (Brooks, 1975). This man, about whom Nixon repeatedly has said, "I would hate to have to get up in the morning and look at his cartoons," has long been an anti-Nixonite. In 1954 his "Here He Comes Now" depicted the then vice-president climbing out of a sewer as a welcoming crowd awaits his arrival (Hess and Kaplan, 1968). Block's location in the nation's capital (*Washington Post*) provides not only an insight into politics but also an audience of the political elite.[3]

Cartoons in the Classroom

The freedom of the press that forms the basis for the liberties taken by editorial cartoonists insures protection for the profession (Conrad, 1975). The current renaissance in political cartooning, precipitated by Watergate, will last as long as objects for derision and reform occupy the American scene. Senator Humphrey (Brooks, 1975) reflected on the contribution of the cartoonists:

> The cartoonist holds up a mirror to society and most of the time we laugh. If we are angered or disheartened by what we see there, we at least should be grateful for the view. If it reflects poorly on our society or our leaders, we should remember the wisdom of cartoonist Walt Kelly: We shall meet the enemy, and he may be us.

Batchelor (Hess and Kaplan, 1968) has suggested that a cartoonist is "a little of the clown, the poet, the historian, the artist, and the dreamer." America's penchant for political abuses coupled with an indigenous sense of humor guarantee that the art of political cartooning and "them damn pictures" will continue to adorn the editorial pages of America's newspapers as one of America's liveliest, enjoyable, and permanent art forms.

The tradition of the political cartoon in America is one of criticism of intolerance, injustice, political corruption, and social evils — a heritage committed to American ideals that have frequently been forgotten. Hopefully, the "word" of cartoonists will be heeded more in the future than it has been in the past (Rose, 1972).

Cartoons, because of their flexibility, lend themselves to many subject areas. They seem particularly useful in some courses: the American presidency, international relations, and national and state government.

Prior to working with cartoons in the classrooms, some ground work is suggested in view of the work of Carl (1968) and Brinkman (1968). The former found that "Newspaper editorial cartoonists are communicating with only a small percentage of the readers"; the latter suggested that because of the problem of interpretation newspapers wishing to influence public opinion should relate the cartoon to the editorial.

Some useful techniques to test comprehension follow:

   (a)   Distribute (or project) a cartoon without a caption and ask the class to suggest one.

(b) Provide the class with a cartoon with a position on one side of the issue and ask the calss to draw a cartoon with a contrary view (stick figures acceptable).

(c) Present two opposing cartoons and ask the class to defend one.

(d) Display an illustration and ask the students to supply a simple explanation of the artist's bias.

The political cartoon offers the potential for the instructor to illustrate a lecture, promote student interaction and discussion, and add humor to the learning process. It holds the promise of helping the student to operate at the higher cognitive levels through creativity and critical thinking. It deserves serious consideration as a teaching strategy by teachers of political science.

The following annotated bibliography offers suggestions for sources of political cartoons:

ABEL, B. (1969) *Best Cartoons of the World from Atlas Magazine.* New York: Dell. Prefaced with an introduction upon the personality of cartoonists, this collection has two chapters of particular value: "The World Cartoonists Look at the U.S.A." and "The World's Cartoonists Look at Politics and Politicians." The carefully chosen cartoons can be used alone or in juxtaposition with an American cartoonist's view of the same event.

Atlas World Press Review. This monthly magazine, (Box 2550, Boulder, CO 80302), published since 1950, contains a regular section entitled "The World in Cartoons." These illustrations taken from newspapers outside this country provide the student of international relations views of how others see us.

BECKER, S. (1959) *Comic Art in America.* New York: Simon and Schuster. Although the main emphasis of this work is comic or humorous, several classic American political cartoons are included. Becker devotes a chapter ("Cabbages and Kings") to political cartoons, emphasizing the development of the political caricature in American history; also included is a treatment of the Pulitzer Prize-winning cartoons. This is a valuable work because of the many illustrations it contains and the discussions of them.

BLOCK, H. (1959) *Herblock's Special for Today.* New York: Simon and Schuster. This is just one of the many collections of cartoons available by one of America's premier contemporary cartoonists. Herblock, presently syndicated in more than 300 newspapers, is a Pulitzer Prize-winning cartoonist whose art stretches over four decades.

BOYD, M. and P. CONRAD (1973) *When in the Course of Human Events.* New York: Sheed and Ward. This collection of well-done cartoons touches everything from Watergate to abortion with accompanying religious quotes. Conrad, one of America's premier contemporary cartoonists, has won the Pulitzer Prize on two occasions.

BROOKS, C. *Best Editorial Cartoons.* Gretna, LA: Pelican. An excellent annual of cartoons from over one hundred cartoonists in the United States and Canada, the collection focuses on the major issues of the year and provides the instructor and students varying cartoonists' viewpoints depending upon their political and geographic biases. Because of its quality it should be a part of every library. All volumes are equally good.

Documentary Photo Aids. Mt. Dora, FL. This small company produces many fine collections of political cartoons useful for posting on bulletin boards (11" x 14"). Examples of cartoon sets available are "Classic American Political Cartoons," "A Cartoon View of Domestic Issues," "Anti-war and Pro-war Cartoons of the First World War," "Cartoons of the Spanish American War," "A Cartoon History of the U.S. Involvement in World War I," "A Cartoon History of U.S. Foreign Policy," "Theodore Roosevelt in Cartoons," "Cartoons of Presidential Elections." Additional collections contain cartoons similar to the above. The selection and quality of the cartoons are excellent.

FITZGERALD, R. (1973) *Art and Politics—Cartoonists of the Masses and Liberator.* Westport, CT: Greenwood. The *Masses* and the *Liberator* were two of the best illustrated radical publications of the early part of this century. This text investigates the work of five socialist artists and contains reprints of sixty cartoons, some of which have become classics.

Foreign Policy Association Editors (1968) *A Cartoon History of United States Foreign Policy.* New York: Vintage. This paperback consists of a collection of political cartoons with a short commentary on each. This fine collection can be used in many courses because of the range of the cartoons (peace, cold war, aggression, diplomacy) and their quality.

HEITZMANN, W. R. (1975) *50 Political Cartoons for Teaching U.S. History.* Portland: Weston Walch. A series of 8½" x 11" posters containing cartoons from Ben Franklin's "Unite or Die" to Edmund Valtman's "Later—My Brother Is Watching" (a commentary on detente). The series, designed to be used from elementary school through graduate school, contains on the reverse side of each poster background to the cartoon and suggestions for use—student learning experiences and questions for discussion. A review appeared in the April 1976 issue of *Teaching Political Science.*

HESS, A. and M. KAPLAN (1968) *The Ungentlemanly Art: A History of American Political Cartoons.* New York: Macmillan. This book is a well-done, nicely narrated sequel to the Nevins-Weitenkampf one, containing several hundred classic cartoons spanning the nation's history. The teacher can benefit from the fine research of the authors. While the analysis and cartoons are nicely meshed, the small size of some of the illustrations mitigates against sharing them with students.

HOHENBERG, J. (1959) *The Pulitzer Prize Story.* New York: Columbia Univ. Press. This work contains reproductions of the cartoons that have been recipients of the Pulitzer Prize; obviously, most are excellent. Among the collection are the works of Fitzpatrick, McCutcheon, Kirby, and Block.

JONES, M. (1971) *The Cartoon History of Britain*. New York: Macmillan (American Edition, 1973). Jones has collected cartoons from 1721 to 1970, giving the teacher an outstanding source of political cartoons. In addition, the work contains commentary on each as well as the development of the cartoon in England. The cartoons are interesting not only because of the opportunity they offer to examine America's early cartoon forms (borrowed from Britain), but also because of the graphic satirical caricatures contained in many.

KELLER, M. (1968) *The Art and Politics of Thomas Nast*. New York: Oxford Univ. Press. This is an outstanding collection of Nast's cartoons which can be reproduced or easily copied. Most cover a large page (8½" x 11"); and several, two pages. The range of subjects treated, the quality of the cartoons, and Nast's influence make this an excellent source for social studies teachers.

LOW, D. (1950) *The Fearful Fifties*. New York: Simon and Schuster. This work, a summary of the decade in England, contains over 100 illustrations on both domestic and international issues. Because of their simplicity, many of the drawings are useful with novice students of editorial cartooning.

MacPHERSON (1972) *Editorial 1972*. Toronto: Toronto Star. A collection of the artist's cartoons from October 1971 to September 1972 that appeared in the *Toronto Star*, the work covers mainly Canadian topics but includes some U.S. subjects.

NEVINS, A. and F. WEITENKAMPF (1933) *A Century of Political Cartoons*. New York: Charles Scribner Sons (republished by Octagon Books). Well-chosen cartoons by an eminent historian and a librarian, the collection covers 1800 to 1900. The cartoons are introduced by an excellent essay analyzing America's cartoon development as well as commenting on the objects of the cartoonists. If one could choose only one collection of America's classic cartoons, this should be it.

OLIPHANT, P. (1973) *Four More Years*. New York: Simon and Schuster. Covering the years from 1969 to 1972, this collection comments on the American scene during those years, devoting much attention to the Nixon-McGovern campaign. Oliphant, both a Pulitzer Prize and Reuben prize winner, has added a short background explanatory comment to some of the illustrations.

PAINE, A. B. (1967) *T. H. Nast — His Period and His Pictures*. Gloucester, MA: Peter Smith. While this analysis of the times and cartoons of Nast contains several fine illustrations, its strength consists in the background and explanation of the cartoons, making it a useful companion to the Keller work. No treatment of political cartoons or cartoonists can exclude America's premier cartoonist.

Political Cartoons. Logan, IA: Perfection Form Co. Ten large (14" x 22") cartoons by Pulitzer Prize winner Frank Miller, these, though probably best used for bulletin board displays, can easily be posted and made reference to during a lecture or discussion. Also available are an additional set of ten by the same artist and a set entitled *Classic Political Cartoons.* The later series contains works by Goldberg, Kirby, Fischetti, and others. Each contains some background information.

SINCLAIR, A. (1962) *Era of Excess—A Social History of the Prohibition Movement.* New York: Harper Colophon. Sinclair's paperback analyzes the Prohibition era, and includes some outstanding political cartoons. The cartoons on bribery and organized crime are particularly useful in contrasting that era with the present.

SPENCER, D. (1949) *Editorial Cartooning.* Ames: Iowa State Univ. Press. Spencer has put together a sort of how its done book with examples from prominent cartoonists. With chapters such as "How the Cartoonist Works," "The Femme and the Pen," and "The History of Editorial Cartooning," he has provided the reader with an interesting and valuable insight to the art.

Understanding Editorial Cartoons. Madison, WI: Visual Education Consultants. This well-done filmstrip explores the technique of the political cartoon, explaining such things as caricature, stereotypes, satire, symbolism, and chiaroscuro. Several fine examples from contemporary cartoonists are shown to illustrate the above concepts.

WILSON, R. R. (1953) *Lincoln in Caricature.* New York: Horizon. Containing 163 cartoons and sketches as well as commentary, this is a useful work for social studies teachers. Included are several illustrations critical of the president as well as several English cartoons which contribute to the quality of the collection. The change in the treatment of Lincoln in the press (June 1860-May 1865) can be ascertained from studying the cartoons.

Notes

[1]Although Thomas Nast dominated cartooning during the latter part of the century, many of his contemporaries gained widespread recognition and influence. This was the era of the expansion of *Harper's Weekly*, which together with *Leslie, Puck, Judge, Life*, and other weeklies, provided an outlet for cartoonists like Walt McDougall ("The Royal Feast of Belshazzar and the Money Kings"), Bernard Gillam ("Phryne before the Chicago Tribune" and "The National Dime Museum"), Joseph Keppler ("Bosses of the Senate"), James A. Wales (" 'Strong' Government 1869-1877, 'Weak' Government 1877-1880"), W. A. Rogers ("The Original Coxey's Army"), Eugene Zimmerman, known as "Zim" ("No Welcome for the Little Stranger"), Grant Hamilton ("Lost!"), and Victor Gillam ("Don Quixote Bryan Meets Disaster in His Fight against Judge's Full Dinner-Pail").

[2]This cartoon was entered as evidence in court following the war when the *Masses* was tried for obstructing the war effort.

[3]It would be remiss not to mention the recent development of a new school of cartoonists who are largely a product of the turbulent 1960s. Exemplified by

Grossman's "LBJ as Santa Claus," in which the former president pictured as Santa Claus is shown laughing as a disfigured Vietnamese child sits in on his lap, the school includes R. O. Blechman, Edward Sorel, and David Levine.

Gary Trudeau ["Doonesbury"] artist and recent Pulitzer Prize recipient, represents another new tradition.

THE COMIC BOOK IS ALIVE AND WELL
AND LIVING IN THE HISTORY CLASS

Alex Dobrowolski

After 11 years of confiscating comic books and badgering offenders who, in their lack of stealth, were caught devouring the frowned-on flotsom of juvenile culture, this year I decided to give my eighth grade American History students an opportunity to thoroughly indulge their appetites without reprimand for a few days. Naturally, there was a price to pay for this seemingly frolicsome adventure. This the students were not to discover until later.

Meanwhile, the objective behind this seemingly mad facade was to *create* comic books rather than read the finished product of another's creation. Since students obtain such delight from these colorful packages of pleasure, why not utilize the basic format which provides them with their unique qualities? The object was to have students identify these qualities and create comic books employing a standard unit in American History. The unit chosen was "Causes of the American Revolution."

Having just completed a unit on the prerevolutionary colonial period, the students were directed, with the utmost sincerity, to bring a comic book of their choice to class the next day. This, of course, raised a number of eyebrows and a flurry of questions but students were purposely not informed that, with the beginning of our study of a new unit, they would become comic book producers. All questions were ignored in favor of maintaining the growing aura of curiosity.

On the appointed day almost 90 percent of my students successfully completed their assignment. All but a still skeptical few brought in their comic books. The new unit already showed promise.

Analyzing the Comic Book's Appeal

Once the class was settled, it was explained to the students how the comic books were to function in this new unit. It was also made clear to them that there was a method behind the outwardly mad scheme. The skeptical few were reassured.

What we did next after outlining the objectives and goals which the comic books were to facilitate was to study quite seriously how a comic book is organized in order to discover its magic appeal. Within a few periods it was the

Reprinted by permission of the author and Heldref Publications from *The Social Studies* 67 (May/June 1976): 118-20, a publication of the Helen Dwight Reid Educational Foundation.

general consensus of the class that most comics follow the same format. The cover is always flamboyant and eye appealing; there is a disclaimer warning readers that none of the material should be taken very seriously; several different stories are housed between the covers, usually following a specific theme such as war, horror, humor, love, or the like; and each story is colorfully illustrated. The class also discovered that advertising takes up a large portion of each comic and that the advertising is geared to a young audience.

The story line was scrutinized carefully also. Many of the comics students brought in had stories which followed distinct patterns. Each story began with a catchy title, then proceeded to introduce the main characters and their problems; these problems then progressed until the main characters found a heroic solution to them. All this was always approached and executed with simplicity. After having carefully dissected the inner workings of a comic it was obvious why comic books held so much appeal. The critical scrutiny was complete.

Organizing for Production

The next step was to organize the class into manageable "editorial staffs." Through a general discussion and assessment of earlier individual student feedbacks, specific talents were identified. The class was divided into six groups with five in a group. Each group included a student who was generally regarded as a good to fair artist (artistic editor), a second student who displayed leadership qualities (managing editor), another who printed well (printing editor), one who had a knack for colors and design (layout editor), and another student who was generally in charge of transposing the facts in the text to comic book form. This person was usually chosen on the basis of his academic abilities and was in charge of maintaining historical accuracy.

Once each group was organized and the various roles and responsibilities were discussed and assigned each team was given its materials. These were 20 sheets of plain ditto paper and one file folder; each group supplied its own coloring pencils and rulers. Later each staff received brass paper fasteners and paper reinforcers.

With the material situation organized, the task at hand was about to begin, but not before basic rules were understood. Each staff was assigned an area in the room and was strictly forbidden to change. However, any one member at any time had the privilege of visting another staff if that foreign staff welcomed his visit. Any staff could choose total privacy at any time.

Time was of the essence. Strict deadlines were established at the outset. The students were given 12 class periods to prepare a minimum 20-page comic book using the text material dealing with the steps which led up to the American Revolution. This involved taking work home and each staff was to decide among themselves who was to take work home and how much.

Grades were not mentioned nor did students raise the topic. Perhaps the nature of the activity precluded the usual inquiries regarding evluation payoffs.

The Production Process

As each staff sorted out the various areas of responsibility, results began to appear. Naturally, some staffs related to each other more positively than others. Some of the difficulty was a matter of direction. Purposely, few specific directions were given, so that each staff was forced to make most of its own decisions.

Students found this frustrating. Apparently most were accustomed to following very specific directions and were surprised to find that now their teacher-directed inquiries were turned back on themselves rather than answered. Within a week most began to turn to their staff for solutions. The comic books were beginning to evolve as true student creations unencumbered by adult prejudices. The experiment was making headway.

At the end of the first week the daily routine took shape. The first few minutes of the class were devoted to a general administrative session. Deadlines were discussed, staff problems aired, and ideas shared. Then the class disbanded into their staff territories with papers, materials, and students interacting dynamically. At about this same time it was discovered that the original deadline was too short. During one of the administrative sessions several staffs urged their fellows and their teacher to modify the schedule. Consequently the deadline was extended to 15 days from the original 12.

Several of the more energetic staffs were able to complete their comics within the deadline. These comics included jazzy covers, appropriate colonial advertising, and of course stories dealing with the different controversial British Acts which were imposed on the colonists and historically led to the American Revolution. Other staffs were in various stages of completion at the deadline.

Evaluating the Product

The next few class periods were devoted to reading each other's comic books and critically assessing their respective virtues. This was done by reassembling staffs and distributing an evaluation instrument to each group designed to rate, on a scale of 1 through 5, the various academic and artistic inputs generated by each staff.

The comics were circulated and each staff gleefully inspected the competition's product. Rating, unfortunately, became for some a weapon rather than a critical evaluation, despite the fact that it was strongly emphasized at the last few general administrative sessions that this was not to be treated as a report card. Students were very critical of each other and at times became totally unfair, losing sight of the original objective. Personalities came into play and fairness at times took a back seat.

However, despite these problems, some positive results were evident. Students were given the opportunity to inspect each other's product and to absorb the various issues involved in the American Revolution. Repetition eased the way towards a better understanding of these issues. Repetition in any other way would have turned students off. In this case they were reviewing each other's work and judging it on the basis of historical accuracy, dialogue, story line, characters, art work, printing, cover, advertising, and supplementary material. In the final analysis, text material can be dull but a comic book can be fun and interesting, especially if it is produced by one's peers.

How Worthwhile Was the Project?

No objective tests were given to evaluate the total unit nor its components. However, student reactions along with a measure of personal bias deserve comment.

Some measure of the success of a project is how much student involvement and commitment takes place in the classroom. This unit equaled almost total involvement. A spontaneous competitive situation grew between the staffs whereby each wanted to produce a better product not for the sake of grades but out of pride in their work.

Each staff had to meet the challenge of transposing text material into comic book format. The formal text material had to be analyzed, synthesized, digested, and rewritten into a simple story with illustrations. Plagiarizing was not accepted. This was probably one of the most valuable aspects of the unit.

Working together for almost a month created mini-communities where students communicated, exchanged ideas, generated new ideas, and generally got to know each other better. Organized into small communities (staffs), individuals learned not only to criticize but also to compromise for the good of the community.

Students at this level need to have their abundant energy harnessed, perhaps more so than any other age group. Any hands-on activity is usually well received. This particular activity encouraged students to create their own hands-on materials in the form of one of the most basic—and therefore most acceptable—aspects of juvenile culture. History under these circumstances can be fun and, to the surprise of the adult, educationally rewarding as well.

ENGLISH CREATE FROM CARTOONS   Neil Vail

"How often should children do creative writing?" That frequently asked question implies that creative writing is apart from conventional, utilitarian-type writing; that creative writing somehow is an unstructured, do-your-own-thing bit. Really, any writing done by child or adult is creative if it has that person's own style in it. Whether ideas come from direct observation of things, people, or events, or whether they come from speech or writings of others, they need not seem trite or imitative if the writer has analyzed and expressed them in his or her own words.

Supplementing this definition of creative writing is the conviction that a writing program can be structured and at the same time creative. Behind each piece of writing there should be a plan. The teacher of composition has a responsibility to develop specific skills throughout the year. Without such preplanning, students will not, other than by happenstance, develop the writing skills that make them competent writers. We can suggest the skills by listing *concreteness, appropriate diction, point of view, consistent tense, progression, sensory impressions, figurative language, subordination and coordination, transitional devices, added detail*, to name but a few. Such skills must be taught specifically if students are to understand them and use them when they write.

Encouraging children to write, of course, requires carefully planned strategies. Motivation, well thought out in advance, pays off. One approach is to show students that everyday happenings can be used for writing stories of interest. For example, bring in a large picture of some event. Perhaps it is a picture of an automobile race with crowds anxiously awaiting the outcome, or a picture of a forlorn child sitting in a barren bus depot. Then talk about it—what does the class see?—and list ideas on the board. Next, determine which ideas can be written, either those pictured or those arising out of the discussion. Care must be taken that students do not merely catalog what they see in the picture. Instead, help them see the germ of a story that they can enlarge upon.

One successful method that some elementary and middle-school teachers use to encourage writers is a device called "cartoon motivators." A single-frame cartoon may be used to help writers develop ideas for a story. Later, a multiple-frame cartoon can provide sequence to a happening and prove useful when more complex writing skills are to be dealt with.

Reprinted from *Instructor* 84 (January 1975): 51-52. Copyright © 1975 by The Instructor Publications, Inc. Used by permission.

The single-frame cartoon reproduced in reduced size here may be used to motivate students to start writing. Have students list some of the things in the scene which they might write about. Note their suggestions on the board, then examine the list to decide what each writer will use. In addition, each writer should select a character (point of view) who will describe all or many of the events in this backyard, perhaps a nosy neighbor, the father or the mother, the dog getting the bath, or one of the other animals. Whoever or whatever is selected to describe the events will, of course, probably omit some of the happenings in this cartoon.

The nosy neighbor might describe with disgust the people next door and what they are doing. Or the father might describe how he had to catch the dog, the trouble he had getting him into the tub, and so on. He also might touch on the other activities in the yard which are disturbing the dog during his bath. Others might want to write from the point of view of the dog being bathed—how he was caught, how he wishes he were "helping" with some of the other activities in the backyard, how he'll get even. The list of characters and events which can be described is long enough for each writer to find something.

Other cartoon sequences can be developed to lead students to see the need for transitional devices, or to become aware of the need for using dialogue, with quotation marks, in a story. Some preteaching of skills, then, is mandatory if the writing lesson is really to be successful.

After students have had some experience with single-frame cartoons, they can be introduced to multiple-frame cartoons that are somewhat open-ended. Such seemingly mundane events as baking a cake while mother is away, a rather congested playground scene, a fisherman being observed from a fish's point of view, the journey of a raindrop, a dandelion seed's adventures, a runaway child's experiences, a sleepwalker, and a trip to the circus, are but a few of the commonplace experiences which can be pictured and which will provide the beginnings for writing.

In using this strategy, help students see that they can insert additional episodes and create new endings. However, focus on the point that they are to incorporate or use the writing objective for that particular lesson in their writing. If the objective for the lesson is to include a detailed description of an object within the context of a story, then evidence of that skill should appear in the finished writing.

To some, giving children the same idea or picture to write about seems wrong since all of the students will turn in the "same theme." As teachers of composition, however, we must realize that although it appears that everyone wrote about the same thing, to the writer his or her theme is unique. Our job is to insure that children learn to write, not that each one initially must have a unique idea about which to write. Once children have become adept at using cartoons to help them create stories, they will quickly learn, with some encouragement, to modify and invent newer and better incidents to write about. Of course we don't expect to use cartoons for every writing assignment. The strategy is but one—albeit a highly effective one—of the very many we may employ to provide motivation.

Once themes have been written, proofed, and recopied, they may be shared orally with the class. If children have similar writing assignments and objectives to meet, they frequently are curious to discover how their peers have tackled the same problems. Sharing themes can help in this.

In addition to reading some of the stories to the class, some should be posted after each writing session. Eventually, be sure that all students have had writings posted. Colorful ribbons with notations such as *good beginning, excellent conclusion, best use of dialogue, unusual title,* and *good word choice* can be attached to these writings to make students proud of what they have done.

Motivating children to want to write can be rewarding not only for the student but for the teacher as well. And careful planning of assignments will result in writing quite different from that of nondirected writers who too often complete assignments not quite sure if they have accomplished what they set out to do.

COMIC BOOKS, HUMOR HELP
LIVEN UP LATIN COURSES

High school students who shudder at the thought of the boring hours they might have to spend in a Latin course may change their minds if a curriculum designed by a University of Illinois professor continues to develop at its present rate.

A new five-year comprehensive classics curriculum for high school students, designed by Dr. Richard Scanlon, professor of classics and secondary education, is being tried out in more than 450 schools throughout the U.S. and Canada. Originally planned for only 40 test schools, the response has skyrocketed so rapidly that Scanlon can barely crank out material fast enough to meet the demand.

To get high school students to tune in on the classics, Scanlon uses a multisensory approach to teaching and relies on the use of visuals to bridge the gap between the student's world and the foreign language.

At the introductory level, the visuals include comic books about "Superlegatus," a Superman figure who rescues a damsel named "Tintinabula" and other ladies from mythological monsters.

The comic books are designed to acquaint the students with both the Latin language and the culture of the times. With this method, Scanlon feels, no dictionaries are required. The student sees the picture and associates it with the word.

While agreeing that the old Caesar-Cicero-Vergil sequence, taught to generations of Americans, is boring for both student and teacher, Scanlon challenges the notion that Latin is dull.

"Students somehow get the idea that no Roman ever smiled or had any fun," he claims. Therefore, he concentrates on making humor a vital element in the curriculum from the start.

Second year Latin, formerly devoted to reading and translating Caesar, has been changed around in Scanlon's curriculum to focus on themes that young people today might find more relevant.

"We discover what various writers thought about war, imperialism, the class struggle of minority groups in ancient Rome, the hero and the anti-hero, religion, philosophy, slavery and the attitudes toward love in ancient times."

The third year, traditionally spent studying the orations of Cicero, in the new curriculum considers the rise and fall of the Roman republic as seen through the eyes of writers of the day.

Students read not only what Cicero, a conservative, thought about the important topics of the day, but also what Sallust, a radical, thought about the same subjects. Students also compare what the Romans themselves thought about their government with the views of modern historians and are encouraged to draw parallels between the Roman republic and government in the U.S. today. In this same year, the study of Greek is introduced, along with a smattering of ancient history and culture.

The fourth year is a study of epic poetry, focusing on the *Aeneid*. The *Illiad* and the *Odyssey*, Dante's *Divine Comedy*, and several Greek tragedies are read in translation, along with such contemporary novels as Mary Renault's *The King Must Die* and *The Bull from the Sea*.

The Latin curriculum program has been funded by the U.S. Office of Education since the fall of 1967, and is now in its second experimental year. Though it's too early to tell whether the new curriculum will result in greatly increased enrollment in Latin classes, Scanlon thinks fragmentary returns from the program's first two years are encouraging.

"The ideas of the classical heritage are so basic to our way of thinking today that they have enormous appeal for the young."

"We should never require Latin," he added, "but we can make it so interesting that students want to take it."

USING COMIC BOOKS TO TEACH READING AND LANGUAGE ARTS

Emma Halstead Swain

Teachers, parents and others concerned about children have criticized comic books for years. Yet, in 1977 approximately 20 million comic books were sold each month in the United States (Knabb 1978), they are popular in many other countries as well, and many professional articles suggest using them in reading and language arts classes (Witty, Smith and Coomer 1942, Ragan and Stendler 1966, Paine 1974, Hallenbeck 1976).

Should materials as plentiful and popular as comic books be used in reading and language arts classes, or will their use expose students to materials read primarily by poor students? Do comic books have no educational value? Can they cause students to lose interest in other types of books? This article examines these questions.

The author collected data for a study on this topic by administering a questionnaire to 169 students in grades four through twelve in Durham, North Carolina. About half the students made good grades in school (an "A" or "B" grade average); the other half made poor grades (a "D" or "Failing" average). To report the findings, students in grades four, five and six will be referred to as elementary school students; students in grades seven, eight and nine will be referred to as junior high students; and students in grades 10, 11 and 12 will be referred to as high school students.

The 169 students who participated in the study included 54 elementary students, 27 who made good grades and 27 who made poor grades; 48 junior high students, 27 who made good grades and 21 who made poor grades; and 67 high school students, 37 who made good grades and 30 who made poor grades.

Popular with Most Students

A large percentage of the participating students in all grades read comic books and/or comic strips (see Table 1). Most of the students who made good grades read comic books. In fact, comic books and/or comic strips were read by more students who made good grades than students who made poor grades. Comic books have a greater appeal to younger students and comic strips to older students. Comic books were read by a larger percentage of participating

Reprinted with permission of the author and the International Reading Association from *Journal of Reading* 22 (December 1978): 253-58.

Table 1

PERCENT OF STUDENTS WHO READ COMIC BOOKS OR COMIC STRIPS

Grade level	Students who read comic books	Students who read comic strips	Students who read comic books and comic strips	Students who now or in the past read comic books
Elementary students who make good grades	96%	96%	100%	—
Elementary students who make poor grades	88	75	89	—
Junior high students who make good grades	51	88	94	77
Junior high students who make poor grades	71	84	90	86
High school students who make good grades	56	92	95	89
High school students who make poor grades	63	79	90	73

elementary school students than by junior high and high school students. A number of the older students who did not read comic books at the time of the study reported they had read them when they were younger. The most common reason older students gave for not reading comic books was lack of time.

Students reported that they had learned many things by reading comic books: new words, that people have imaginations, how a ship finder works, jokes, how to take the venom out of snakes, how to read and spell better, draw, and make money. They learned about comedy, history, people, the supernatural, Abraham Lincoln, nuclear theory, planets, animals, karate, football, and different places around the world. Students who read comic books said they had not lost interest in reading other types of books: 91% of the students who made good grades and 79% of the students who made poor grades reported they read library books as well as comic books.

The data suggest that using comic books and/or comic strips in reading and language arts classes may be an effective strategy in that most students like to read them, they are educational, and they do not discourage students from reading other types of books.

Comics in the Classroom

The following list provides 20 suggestions for reading and language arts activities using comic books or comic strips. Recommended grouping is also noted, i.e., entire class, small group, partners, individual.

- *Consonant Blends.* Have students copy from a comic book five words that contain a consonant blend. Entire class, small group, individual.
- *Picture Interpretation.* Using one frame from a comic book or comic strip, have students circle each word that refers to something in the picture and draw a line from the word to the item it refers to. Entire class, small group, individual.
- *Special Print.* Using an advertisement in a comic book, have students find examples of words in a larger or different style of type. Discuss why the advertiser wanted to emphasize these words. Entire class, small group.
- *Possessives.* Using an advertisement in a comic book, have students choose one item each for three friends and write their names in possessive form over the item. Small group, partners.
- *Compound Words.* Have students find and circle as many compound words as possible in a comic book story, then select five of the words and use them in sentences. Small group, partners.
- *Antonyms.* List ten words and have students find pictures in comic strips that mean the opposite of each word. They should cut out the picture and write the antonym on it. Small group, partners, individual.
- *Following Directions.* Use a comic book that contains an advertisement with an order blank. Have students fill out the order, pretending they have five dollars to spend. Entire class, small group, individual.
- *Reading for Details.* Have students read a comic book story, then close the book and list as many details of the story as possible. Individual.
- *Summarization.* Have students write a one-sentence summary of a comic strip. Small group, individual.
- *Detecting Mood.* Using a comic strip or comic book, have students find pictures that represent the mood of a sweepstakes winner, a person who lost a tennis match, a person at a birthday party, or a person who has just seen a snake. Small group, partners.
- *Predicting Outcome.* Provide students with all the frames of a comic strip except the last one and ask them to draw the last frame. Partners, individual.
- *Major and Minor Characters.* Using a comic book or comic strip, have students circle the major characters and underline the minor ones, then discuss the differences. Entire class, small group.
- *Character Quotes.* Using a comic book or comic strip, have students identify a character type such as bully or star athlete and find an example of something the character might say. Partners, individual.
- *Characterization.* Have students select the central character of a comic book or comic strip and choose one adjective that would describe that character. Then find five things the character did or said in the story to support the choice.

- *Alphabetical Order.* Have students cut apart a page of comic strips, then rearrange them according to alphabetical order of titles. Small group, partners, individual.
- *Classification.* Using different kinds of comic books, have students divide the books into categories such as comedy, love, superhero, etc.
- *Main Idea.* Use any comic book that does not have a caption on the front page. Have students write captions expressing main idea for the front page. Partners, individual.
- *Critical Reading — Fantasy.* Have students list all the clues in a comic book story that tell them the story is not realistic and could not possibly happen. Small group, partners.
- *Critical Reading — Persuasion.* Have students find three or four advertisements in a comic book and cross out any emotional or persuasive words.
- *Figurative Language.* Have students find as many slang words as possible in a comic book or group of comic strips and define the words using context clues. Small group, partners.

Any number of comic book and comic strip reading activities can be developed. All a teacher needs is a list of reading skills to be developed, a box of comic books, and a collection of comic strips. However, be careful of one thing: make sure the activities focus the students' attention on the words, not the pictures. Otherwise, the poorer readers may spend their time on non-reading aspects of the activity (Arlin and Roth 1978).

In order to be sure the comic books and comic strips will be appropriate for the students who will be working with them, teachers should ask their students some questions. What comic books do they like to read? What comic book and comic strip characters do they like to read about? What comic books are easy and what comic books are difficult for them to read? Since some teachers may have difficulty collecting this information, Table 2 [page 76-77] lists the preferences of the American students included in this study.

References

Arlin, Marshall and Garry Roth. "Pupils' Use of Time while Reading Comics and Books." *American Educational Research Journal*, vol. 5, no. 2 (Spring 1978), pp. 201-16.

Hallenbeck, Phyllis N. "Remediating with Comic Strips." *Journal of Learning Disabilities*, vol. 9 (January 1976), pp. 11-15.

Knabb, Kenneth. Telephone interview, March 8, 1978.

Paine, Carolyn A. "Comics for Fun and Profit." *Learning*, vol. 3, no. 2 (October 1974), pp. 86-89.

Ragan, William B. and Celia Burns Stendler. *Modern Elementary Curriculum.* New York, N.Y.: Holt, Rinehart and Winston, 1966.

Witty, Paul, Ethel Smith and Anne Coomer. "Reading the Comics in Grades VII and VIII." *The Journal of Educational Psychology*, vol. 33 (1942), pp. 173-82.

Table 2

INFORMATION FOR DESIGNING COMIC BOOK AND COMIC STRIP ACTIVITIES

Grade level	Features that help students read comic books	What students like best about comic books	Favorite comic book characters	Favorite comic strip characters	Comic books that are easy to read	Comic books that are difficult to read
Elementary students who make good grades	Pictures Easy words Suspense Action Captions	Characters Stories Illustrations Announcements Advertisements	Archie Hulk Richie Rich Captain America Spiderman	Dennis The Menace Charlie Brown Nancy Snoopy Blondie	Archie Richie Rich Superman Sad Sack Yogi Bear	Love Story Hulk Avengers Batman UFO
Elementary students who make poor grades	Pictures Easy words Large print Title Layout	Illustrations Characters Stories Announcements Advertisements	Hulk Superman Batman Spiderman Archie	Fred Flintstone Henry Snoopy Family Circus Charlie Brown	Archie Love Story Mickey Mouse Richie Rich Casper	Superman Spiderman Hulk Batman Mad
Junior high students who make good grades	Pictures Large print Captions Comedy Plot	Characters Illustrations Stories Letters to the Editor Announcements	Archie Spiderman Richie Rich Superman Avengers	Dennis The Menace Snoopy Charlie Brown Family Circus Kerry Drake	Archie Richie Rich Casper Yogi Bear Sergeant Fury	Superman Love Story

Junior high students who make poor grades	Pictures Title Easy words Action Characters	Characters Illustrations Stories Announcements Letters to the Editor	Batman Charlie Brown Archie Spiderman Richie Rich	Henry Dennis The Menace Blondie Nancy Snoopy	Charlie Brown Richie Rich Archie Love Story Popeye	Superman Spiderman Dick Tracy Zombie
High school students who make good grades	Pictures Characters Facial expressions Easy words Captions	Illustrations Characters Stories Letters to the Editor Advertisements	Archie Superman Richie Rich Captain America Batman	Dennis The Menace Charlie Brown Blondie Nancy Family Circus	Archie Richie Rich Love Story Charlie Brown Dennis The Menace	Superman Spiderman Fantastic Four
High school students who make poor grades	Pictures Captions Easy words Large print Action	Characters Illustrations Stories Advertisements Announcements	Superman Batman Charlie Brown Ironman Popeye	Dennis The Menace Henry Family Circus Charlie Brown Snoopy	Archie Charlie Brown Casper Popeye Marmaduke	Superman Spiderman Fantastic Four Six Million Dollar Man

II

HOW?

- activities for use in the exercise of oral, listening, reading, writing, and vocabulary skills

- for building language skills—steps for students to follow in comic strip word study

- with learning centers to provide opportunities for skill-building, creativity, and reading

- suggestions on how to use comic books for learning

- to provide useful and appealing material for reading comprehension activities

FOUR-COLOR WORDS: COMIC BOOKS IN THE CLASSROOM

Robert N. Schoof, Jr.

> There is statistical evidence that even in this latter day of domination by television, well over 90 percent of American children still read comic books—and perhaps more surprisingly—approximately 50 percent of American *adults* do the same.
>
> —Dick Lupoff
> —Don Thompson

Just what is there about comic books that is so attractive to children? More than a few teachers, while browsing through forbidden comic books confiscated during math or social studies, have puzzled over the attraction of the never-ending advertisements for muscle-building apparatus and switch-blade combs, the outrageous drawings depicting leotarded heroes and heroines battling the hideous forces of evil, or the constantly recurrent theme of evil almost triumphant, but always defeated in the final cliff-hanging moment. Why is it that oftentimes children who appear totally uninterested in reading school materials will claim with pride to have not missed a single issue of *Spider-Man* or *Wonder Woman* in months? What is there about these colorful little magazines, so often dismissed as poorly printed, cheap bits of sensationalism, that children find so attractive?

In the end, probably the only answer to this question is simply that for most children and even for many adults, comic books are "fun" to read. The stories, characters, and format are compelling and accessible to juvenile perceptions. And since verbal descriptions and dialogue are, by the very nature of the medium, always accompanied by illustrations, they are easily comprehended by even poor readers. An additional plus lies in the amount of time required for their reading—from ten to twenty minutes, in most cases, depending on individual reading ability. And finally, even at the current inflationary price of thirty-five cents, comic books are still affordable to almost everyone—children included.

While it is true that comic books are printed on the cheapest of paper, are hardly lettered consistently, and usually include stories and advertisements that seem overly sensational to adult sensibilities, it is also true that most children aren't bothered by this in the least. There is still something about comic books that attracts kids the way Batman attracts villains. Devotion such as this, to any kind of reading, should hardly be ignored. It would seem that, if for no reason other than for this ability to stimulate interest in reading, comic books are definitely worth consideration as potentially valuable teaching tools.

Speaking as one who first learned to love reading through comic books, I believe that they can be put to good use in the classroom. Comic books can be effectively utilized for the exercise of almost all aspects of the language arts program, with an added capacity to generate student interest often absent in standard school reading materials.

The activities that follow represent ten possibilities for the use of comic books in the exercise of oral, listening, reading, writing, and vocabulary skills. They are designed for use at the upper elementary or middle-school levels, but could be easily adapted for use with younger or older students.

1. The "Who's Who" of Comic Books

Compiling a comic book "Who's Who" as a class project not only serves to acquaint students with the major comic book characters, but also provides an interesting means for the practice of descriptive writing and research skills.

To prepare for this activity, the instructor should cut out as many pictures from old comic books as there are students in the class, and mount them on separate sheets of construction paper. These should include pictures of major comic book characters, places, vehicles, weapons, etc., and should be clearly labeled. After the sheets have been distributed to the class (one per student), the characters should be investigated and a paragraph or two written on each sheet describing the character's (or thing's) physical characteristics, super powers, weaknesses, and other traits. The instructor will, of course, be responsible for directing the students to the appropriate resource materials for this information. These could consist of old comic books, or any of the paperback anthologies of old comic books currently available (see references).

Upon completion, the sheets should be arranged alphabetically, signed by the students, dated, and placed in a binding or file box for easy reference. This book or file then, can be kept in the classroom to be used as a basic source of comic book information, both for the present and for future classes.

2. Telling a Book by Its Cover

Instead of researching the characters, as in the previous activity, the students might be expected to theorize about their personalities, and to write brief, speculative character studies based on the pictures alone.

The instructor should begin, as before, by distributing sheets on which are mounted pictures of various comic book characters. For this activity, it is preferable that only character sheets with which the students are unfamiliar be distributed. Based on the pictures, the students should write brief descriptions focusing on the characters' moods, possible thoughts, emotions, and backgrounds. The objective is not physical description, but rather speculation based only on the pictures of what goes on within the characters.

This activity furnishes an opportunity for students to use their imaginations, and to write creatively in a manner they will find highly motivational. After sharing the descriptions with each other, the students will probably wish to investigate the characters, as in the previous activity, to determine how close their character descriptions came to the intentions of the original creators.

3. Introducing the Concept of Dialect

Comic book characters rarely speak the Queen's English. Ironically, often times the only characters who do speak precise English in comic books are the mad-scientist-villain types. This use of dialect gives the characters an added depth of personality often missing in standard reading text characters, and makes possible the development of a more personal relationship between reader and subject. Comic books have real value, then, for introducing the concept of dialectal spellings and pronunciations.

It is essential that students understand from the outset, however, that the dialectal passages serve a purpose and are not mistakes. The best way to illustrate this is to assign parts and read a comic book out loud. The reasoning behind the apparent misspellings becomes clear when students hear the words pronounced in their proper contexts. Discussion should also continually accompany the reading: "What kind of person would we expect to speak this way?" "What does the character's speech reveal about his or her background and personality?" "What are some dangers in making assumptions about character from speech?"

Follow-up activities could include a study of the dialectal writings of Mark Twain, or involvement of the students in writing examples of dialect with which they themselves are familiar.

4. Comic Character Creation

Another activity, useful for the exercise of descriptive writing skills, consists of having the students actually create their own comic book characters.

It is essential for this activity that students give physical descriptions of their characters with accompanying drawings. But beyond this, a great deal of psychological and emotional description is necessary for the realization of truly complete characters. The more detail and background information given about the characters, the better.

Upon completion, each student should share his or her creation with the rest of the class. These characters can later be incorporated into a class comic book, if desired.

5. Creating Character Names

A natural extension of the preceding activity that can be instrumental in helping students to understand how words originate is to have them invent names for their creations.

One way to start is for each student to blend together words that best describe his or her character. For example: brains + strength = "Braingth" — a hero who not only can leap tall buildings in a single bound, but who also can design them. For the half-man, half-bear character, "Bearan" might be suitable.

Another possibility would be for the students to explore the strident or pleasant aspects of various sounds in determining the qualities that would best reflect the personalities of their characters. "Ekpit," for example, might be a good name for a garbage-eating monster, as opposed to a name like "Mayla," which obviously wouldn't fit this character at all. The possibilities here are endless.

This activity could easily develop into a study of the names created by J. R. R. Tolkien in his middle-earth fantasies. Tolkien invented entire langauges and was a master at assigning his characters appropriate names. Examples include: "Beorn"—the bear-man, "Bilbo"—the Hobbit, "Smaug"—the fire-breathing dragon, and "Morgoth"—the arch villain.

At the very least, this activity can help to instill within the student a greater awareness of how words and names originate. Even if the resulting awareness is somewhat vague and incomplete, at least it represents an enjoyable beginning.

6. *Making Characters out of Students* (hardly necessary)

A further variation of the character description theme is for the students to imagine that they are comic book heroes and heroines themselves. Each student should select one talent or special ability that he or she possesses and develop it into the main feature of the character's strength. An example would be the student who is an accomplished baseball player. How could this special ability be used to "save the day"? Or how could the student who likes to sew, sew his or her way out of a dangerous situation? This technique of singling out a specific talent and magnifying it to super-human proportions is a standard method for the creation of new comic book characters.

Of course, as in the previous activities, written descriptions of the characters will be important. But the students will derive additional enjoyment from writing follow-up stories in which, for example, "Super-Sewer" saves the day, and then sharing these with each other. This focusing of attention on the individual strengths of each student will help to promote a deeper awareness and understanding of each individual's intrinsic value as a human being.

7. *Dramatic Adaptation*

The dramatization of a comic book story is a major and definitely worthwhile venture. Dramatization focuses attention primarily on oral and listening skills through group organization, rehearsal, discussion, and performance. Reading and writing skills are also involved, though to a lesser degree. The productions can range from simple, one-act comic strip plays presented within the class, to elaborate comic book productions, complete with scenery, costumes and sound effects.

Before attempting the dramatization of an entire comic book, it's a good idea to have small groups of students experiment with comic strips. The demands presented by the dramatization of an entire comic book will probably exceed the abilities of the students (and teacher) at first. After several successful attempts at comic strips, however, the more elaborate production of an entire comic book may be attempted.

Of the multitude of details involved in such a project, several stand out as being of primary importance. The first obstacle to overcome will be the need to adapt the comic strip (or book) format to that of a presentable dramatic play. Dialogue, of course, can be lifted directly from the original text, though production and scenery information will need to be written up. The presentations should be kept as simple as possible at first, with no costuming, and only basic props. More elaborate costuming and scenery may be attempted when everyone is more familiar with the process. Sound effects will need to be simulated. Students should experiment with various materials to determine which sounds most closely approximate the sounds of hoofbeats, motor noises, and ray-gun blasts. If available and willing, local T.V. or radio personnel could be of great assistance here. Finally, character roles will have to be established, rehearsals organized, and an audience secured. The presentation may be as simple or as complicated as time and students' abilities permit.

The process of preparing for such a performance affords the students considerable first hand experience with the give and take of constructive criticism, in addition to fostering a deeper understanding of the possibilities inherent in group work.

8. Reversing the Roles

Over the years, the anti-feminine bias traditionally associated with comic books has practically disappeared. In fact, at present there are almost as many female characters as there are male. Always seeking a wider audience, comic book publishers have taken strides toward balancing what has traditionally been a male-centered medium. At present, however, comic book writers (most of whom are male) are in the awkward position of trying to determine how the new heroines should behave—with the unfortunate result that many of their experiments don't at all resemble what most girls would hope for in a "super-female" character.

An interesting way to examine these expectations and biases is for the students to act out a comic book with all the major roles reversed. The heroes will now become heroines, and vice versa. The true test lies in determining if any factors beside the role changes will have to be altered to make for a realistic story and realistic characters. What can be said about our expectations if changes are found to be necessary? Would a female character who talks and acts like a man be realistic? What part does tradition play in deciding this? What about the man who talks and acts like a woman? Are traditional roles justifiable, or not?

The purpose of this activity is simply to promote an awareness and questioning of traditional role expectations that the students may not even be aware they possess. Comic books provide an excellent stimulus for this kind of examination.

9. "Sound-Words"

Sounds in comic books are usually represented by an extreme form of onomatopoeia (*Sok!, Screech!, Skarakkk!, Bwok!*). Comic book writers seem to delight in creating the most unusual sound representations possible. Students will likewise enjoy trying their hands at creating "sound-words," and in the process will gain a greater awareness of how many of our standard onomatopoeic words originated.

The instructor should begin by presenting various situations for which a comic book writer would have to create "sound-words." Sound effects records or tape-recorded noises would be helpful here, though not essential. The student should then invent corresponding words for each of the noises or noise-producing situations. Finally, these should be listed on the board and compared, with each student pronouncing his or her own words out loud.

10. *Student-Made Comic Books*

In small groups, the students should now attempt to write and draw their own comic books. This is definitely an enormous undertaking, requiring considerable time for preparation and execution. Approaching it as a group rather than as an individual activity, however, will smooth things out considerably. Comic books are never produced by single individuals, but rather by teams of writers, artists, colorists and lettering specialists. This basic team framework is also a very efficient way to organize students for such a project.

The first step will be for each group to either write its own story, or to select one with which its members are already familiar. Probably the only realistic way in which such a story will ever be successfully written by an entire group is for each member to write a short adventure involving a pre-determined central character, and then to combine these adventures to form the basic story-line ("The Adventures of ... "). A preferable alternative, however, might be for each group to simply select a particular myth or fable, and then to translate this into the comic book format. The heroes of classic Greek, Roman, and Norse mythology make tremendous comic book heroes.

After the stories have been selected or written, they should be re-written as scripts, and then drawn as comic books. Drawing and writing chores should be shared among group members. Two or three students can be responsible for the script. One student can do the lettering, another the outlining, etc.

Finally, upon completion each group should present its creation to the class, with group members reading the various parts aloud. An opaque projector is practically essential here, unless the class is particularly small or the comic books particularly large.

Concealed within this one activity is the capacity for exercising several important aspects of the language arts program. Reading and writing skills, for example, will be used in preparing the initial story for comic book adaptation. Oral and listening skills will be exercised through discussion, group participation, cooperation, and presentation. But best of all, even though this activity does much to exercise important language development skills, the students will be having too much fun to ever realize it.

To anyone who remembers the "crime" comic books of the thirties and forties, these activities may be hard to accept. The crime comics coupled intense violence with sexual overtones, and were definitely not suitable for classroom use. In a 1953 study by psychiatrist Fredric Wertham, these comic books were closely examined and found to present a real threat to the mental hygiene of children who read them. Dr. Wertham's study, described in his book *Seduction of the Innocent*, is probably the major reason for the improvements in comic books that have come about in the last twenty years. Unfortunately though, this same study has also had the effect of blinding many parents and educators to the positive aspects of the more recent comic books.

There have been great improvements in comic books over the last twenty years. The stories found in modern comic books often express values that would have been inconceivable in the crime comics of the thirties and forties. Touching family scenes, for example, can regularly be found in the ever-popular *Fantastic Four*. Spider-Man, who in real life is a student, has to study diligently between his adventures. The villains found in today's comic books are seldom hopelessly evil, but are usually driven by some unfortunate character defect such as pride or greed. And finally, the violence found in modern comic books never includes blood, and rarely if ever, death. In fact, when compared with the violence children are exposed to on television, one hesitates to call modern comic books violent at all.

This is not to say that all comic books are suitable for classroom use. The muscle-building advertisements and the exaggerated physical aspects of the drawings still might occasionally prove unsuitable, depending on the make-up of local community standards. This is simply a matter of teacher discretion. The existence of an occasionally objectionable comic book, however, shouldn't rule out the possibility of their use in the classroom any more than one or two biased textbooks would eliminate the use of all textbooks in the classroom.

Finally, comic books should never be expected to serve as art or literature. That is not their purpose, and never has been. In a sense, comic books are still nothing more than entertaining junk (see Feiffer 1965) — but junk with a potential value. Their capacity to entertain children is every bit as strong as that of Saturday morning T.V. shows, or any of the other programs and movies that children find entertaining. But comic books possess an added property usually missing in other forms of popular juvenile entertainment: they need to be *read!* Comic books are not by any means the solution to all language and reading problems. But in this day of increasing apathy toward the printed word, and ever-growing loyalty to the television screen, they can, with a little imagination, spark interest where other reading and language development materials fail.

References

Feiffer, Jules. *The Great Comic Book Heroes.* New York: The Dial Press, 1965.

Lee, Stan. *Origins of Marvel Comics.* New York: Simon & Schuster, 1974.

_____. *Son of Origins of Marvel Comics.* New York: Simon & Schuster, 1975.

_____. *Bring on the Bad Guys*. New York: Simon & Schuster, 1976.

_____. *The Superhero Women*. New York: Simon & Schuster, 1977.

O'Neil, Dennis, ed. *Secret Origins of the Super D.C. Heroes*. New York: Warner Books, 1976.

Reitberger, Reinhold, and Fuchs, Wolfgang. *Comics: Anatomy of a Mass Medium*. Boston: Little, Brown and Company, 1971.

Thompson, Don, and Lupoff, Dick eds. *The Comic-Book Book*. New Rochelle: Arlington House, 1973.

Tolkien, John Ronald Reuel. *The Hobbit*. New York: Ballantine Books, Inc., 1966.

_____. *The Return of the King*. New York: Ballantine Books, Inc., 1965.

Wertham, Fredric. *Seduction of the Innocent*. New York: Rinehart & Company, Inc., 1954.

WORD STUDY: COMIC STRIP STYLE

Elfrieda C. Pierce

Often the whole point of a comic strip hinges on the understanding of a key word. And while providing for heightened enjoyment of comic strips is not a major objective of school, building language skills is—and thereby hangs on activity.

Clip and collect comics and cartoons that, besides being appealing, include challenging and useful words that could enrich and enhance student vocabularies. In each strip or cartoon underline a key word in color.

Steps for students to follow in comic strip word study might include the following:

1. You'll need a comic strip and a sheet of construction paper. (Read the comic strip; do you get the joke?)

2. Read through the rest of these directions to see what you'll be doing and how much space you'll need.

3. Paste the comic strip on the paper.

4. Below the comic strip, copy the word that is underlined in color.

5. Find the word in your dictionary. Show on your paper the way the word is pronounced, and write its definition.

6. Use the word in two sentences of your own. Try to think of sentences that help to show what the word means.

7. Color the cartoon or decorate the paper if you'd like—so that other people will want to look at and read your paper.

Note: If this is to be an independent activity at a learning station, you may want to establish a blind "grab-bag"—type procedure for picking a comic strip—so people won't read through all the comics before selecting one. It just isn't as much fun to use the papers for a display later if the jokes are already old and familiar to everyone.

This sort of attention to cartoon vocabulary may interest students in helping resupply your store of cartoons for later use. And some of your more reluctant readers may find themselves reading these posted comics with new understanding and enjoyment.

Reprinted by permission of the author and *Learning*, The Magazine for Creative Teaching, November 1977. Copyright © 1977 by Pitman Learning, Inc.

FUN, FUNNY, FUNNIES

Trudy Urbani

For just pennies a week any teacher can have fresh, effective learning materials daily and a colorful bonus each weekend. This apparent miracle is accomplished by establishing a multidisciplinary center that uses the funnies as facilitators in the classroom. Comic strips provide practically everything needed to make the year interesting, colorful and fun.

Providing opportunities for skill-building, creativity and reading for content as well as for pleasure are major objectives of the "Funny Paper Center." Most children are already hooked on reading the comics. All you have to do is channel this interest into a broad range of content areas. "Andy Capp" might be expanded into a unit on England. In "Hi and Lois" the baby Trixie is a perfect taking-off point for learning such concepts as cycles, change and cause and effect. "Peanuts" is a priceless commodity for teaching human relations. "Dennis the Menace," "B.C.," "Blondie" and others often deal with mathematics, science and social studies. All can be used for specific language arts, reading and thinking skills. The possibilities are endless.

The Funnies Place

A permanent cartoon center set up in your classroom can be your basic group teaching tool as well as a concept reinforcer for individual children. A couple of weeks before you launch the center, ask your students to bring as many newspaper cartoons as possible from home. Let these pile up and you'll have plenty of working materials. One copy of the newspaper delivered to the classroom daily and kept at the center will keep students up to the minute on their favorite cartoons (as well as current events) and help motivate enthusiasm for the center. As the center is in use have your students continually replenish the comic strip supply.

Several pages of the Sunday comics, glued to three panels of ceiling tile or three large pieces of stiff cardboard, will form an inexpensive decorative triptych for use as a center background. Here you can post activities and storage envelopes. And on a table nearby place other activity cards with stacks of funny papers needed to do the required work. After you decide on your activities, write student direction cards, laminate them and mount them on dark construction

Reprinted from *Teacher* 96 (September 1978): 60-62, 64, 66, 68. Copyright © by Macmillan Professional Magazines. Used by permission of The Instructor Publications, Inc.

paper so they will stand out against your colorful triptych. Also laminate those comics that can carry their own directions or that need to be reused with particular activities. The remaining comics can remain "as is." You'll also need paper, scissors, felt-tip pens (including some in light colors for highlighting), paste, crayons, dictionaries and thesauri.

Comics Activities

The following activities are some that I have tried. They encompass a variety of learning levels, but many can be scaled up or down for older or younger children. I introduce the funny paper activities to younger students in groups. Older learners need less initial direction. As you develop your own activities, be sure to evaluate each to make certain your objectives have been met.

Student evaluation can be accomplished through art presentation, self-checking answer keys, teacher's helpers or teacher observation. Group discussion and interaction are other valuable means of evaluation. Completed projects can be posted on a sharing bulletin board so all may benefit.

1—Funnies Language Arts

- Phonetic Analysis
  Objective: To practice spelling and phonics skills.
  Student directions: "Use a highlighter to mark all comic strip words that contain consonant blends. Cut out the words you have marked and, devoting a column to each blend, paste the words on a sheet of paper."
  Variation: Ask students to search for digraphs or words beginning with consonants.

- Vocabulary
  Objective: To practice dictionary skills and increase vocabulary.
  Student directions: "Search for words you don't know the meaning of and list them. Look them up in the dictionary and write a definition."
  Extension: Ask students to finish off their dictionary definitions by adding synonyms from a thesaurus.

- Root Words
  Objective: To reinforce the concept of root words.
  Student directions: "Highlight words that have prefixes and suffixes and underline the root with a red pencil. Write down each root and other words that contain it."
  Variations: Ask students to highlight contractions and then write them with the two components they stand for on another paper. Or, have them do this with compound words.

- Alphabetization
  Objective: To practice using alphabetical order.
  Student directions: "Cut out a number of comic strip titles. Mix these in a box. Pull out three and paste them in alphabetical order on paper. Repeat the exercise until all the titles are used."

- Silent Letters

  Objective: To recognize how often words contain letters that are not pronounced.

  Student directions: Highlight words that contain silent letters (examples might include *e, k, g* and *m*) and cut them out. Group these by letter and paste them on a sheet of paper.

- Fabricated Words

  Objective: To practice observation skills for recognizing made-up or portmanteau words.

  Student directions: "Make a list of words that have been created for a particular comic strip. Examples might be *vantastic, splendiforous* and *terrorific.* Write down the purpose you think each word serves."

- Catagorization

  Objective: To learn to organize by theme.

  Student directions: "Search the comics for words pertaining to sports, health, geography, science or other themes you identify. Cut out the words for one theme and make a collage. You might want to include pictures."

- Story Lines

  Objective: To think creatively and practice story construction.

  Student directions: "Cut two sheets of plain paper in half widthwise. Stack the four pieces and fold and staple them like a book. Now create your own story by cutting out pictures of cartoon characters from several different comics and arranging them—one frame per page—to form a narrative. Write in dialog near the characters' heads, and draw a 'balloon' around each block of speech with a point coming from the mouth of the character speaking the words."

- Proofreading

  Objective: To practice proofreading and improve punctuation and capitalization skills.

  Student directions: "Highlight all the punctuation, such as periods, commas, apostrophes, quotation marks, question marks and exclamation marks, in one comic strip. Circle all words that are capitalized. Think about the reasons for the punctuation and capitalization and discuss them with a friend."

- Synopsis

  Objective: To be able to briefly outline a story, indicating the beginning, middle and end.

  Student directions: "Write down a brief description of a cartoon story sequence. Be sure your synopsis has a beginning, middle and end. Have a friend write a synopsis of the same cartoon. Compare your efforts. Can you write a better story description using both?"

- And In the Next Episode ...

  Objective: To develop creative writing skills.

  Student directions: "Let your imagination soar. Draw and write an original next episode for one of the comic strips in today's paper. Make a good copy and post it on the sharing bulletin board. Tomorrow compare *your* continuation with the one the cartoonist did and with some your classmates did."

- Story Analysis

   Objective: To develop the ability to read for meaning.

   Student directions: "Read 'Doonesbury,' 'Tank McNamara' or 'Funky Winkerbean.' See if you can figure out what point the cartoonist is making."

2—Funnies Math

- Story Problems

   Objective: To practice choosing the correct operation to solve a story problem.

   Student directions: "Make up a math story problem from a cartoon story line. For example: If Beetle Bailey has hiked 40 miles on a day when the Sarge ordered a 50-mile hike, how far does Beetle still have to go? Write out your problem. After it write the operation (addition, subtraction, multiplication or division) or operations a classmate will have to use to solve the problem. Store it in the 'Cartoon Story Problem' box."

- Graphing

   Objective: To make a four-bar bar graph.

   Student directions: "Take one daily comic section. Cut out all the strips and sort them into one-, two-, and four-frame piles. Make a bar graph that shows the number of strips that have one, two, three and four frames."

- Time

   Objective: To practice telling time by reading clocks and watches and to develop observation skills by using clues to ascertain the time of day or the season of the year.

   Student directions: "Check some comics for clocks, watches or other clues that give you an idea of what time of day it is. On a piece of paper, write the cartoon titles and dates and draw clock faces to indicate what time it is in each cartoon. Also use your observation skills, checking weather signs or clothing worn to try to identify the season of the year. Write the season under the clock face. Check your decisions with the teacher or a friend."

- Numerals

   Objective: To reinforce the concepts of numeral recognition and column addition.

   Student directions: "On a full page of cartoons find and circle all numerals with a red pencil. Write them in order in a column and add them up."

- Measurement

   Objective: To practice measuring skills.

   Student directions: "Measure three cartoons of varying lengths with a regular ruler. Now measure each again using a metric ruler. Note the differences."

   Variation: Figure the total area of any one comic strip in inches and centimeters.

- Geometry

  Objective: To practice recognition skills pertaining to geometric shapes.

  Student directions: "With a red pencil or marking pen go through one of the daily comic strips and circle the circles, trace the triangles, box the squares and trace the rectangles."

3 — Funnies Science

- Classifying

  Objective: To reinforce the concept of classification.

  Student directions: "Cut a group of daily comics into individual strips. Sort them according to any of the following categories or a category of your choice: sports; one, two, three or four panels; one-word titles; women in titles; titles with alliteration; comics with 'balloons' and those without; indoor versus outdoor action; military; political satire; contemporary; animals; careers; family humor; historical; fantasy; women's lib; true-to-life. Write your classification label on a piece of paper and clip it and the strips together for our 'Cartoon Interests' box."

- Sequencing

  Objective: To practice interpreting data.

  How to make: Cut out one comic strip. Paste it on construction paper and then laminate it. Number the panels in order on the back for self-checking. Cut them apart. Prepare other strips in the same way. Keep each set in an envelope.

  Student directions: "Choose an envelope, remove the comic strip frames and, after you turn them all face up, mix them. Now put the pieces in the proper order. Turn them over and check the numbers to see whether you have sequenced the strip correctly."

- Sound Effects

  Objective: To develop an awareness of the sounds in the environment.

  Student directions: "Using two pieces of paper cut in half, folded together and stapled in the center, prepare a 'Noisy Book.' Illustrate it with such comic-strip noise words as *zap, boom* and *honk*. Paste the words and accompanying pictures in the book or paste in only the words and draw in your own pictures."

- Five Senses

  Objective: To reinforce an awareness of the senses.

  Student directions: "Cut out sight, sound, touch, taste and smell words. Label a paper with these headings and paste each word on it under the proper heading."

- Animal Hunt

  Objective: To analyze the characteristics of animals and develop research skills.

  Student directions: "Cut out five cartoon frames each showing a different animal. Using books in our library for research, write a few sentences about the characteristics of each. Then write some contrasts and comparisons."

4—Funnies Social Studies

- You and Me

  Objective: To develop self-awareness.

  Student directions: "Find a cartoon character who is about your age. Compare your looks and actions to his or hers. Name three things you like about your cartoon character. Name three things you like about yourself."

- Feelings

  Objective: To practice recognizing and controlling emotions.

  Student directions: "Look for cartoons in which characters are mad, sad or glad. What action is causing these reactions? What brings out these feelings in you? We'll get a group together to discuss all of our feelings."

- Ethnic Studies and Geography

  Objectives: To develop an awareness of the likenesses and differences in people of different ethnic backgrounds and competency in the areas of map, globe and research skills.

  Student directions: "Read such strips as 'Andy Capp,' 'Wizard of Id' and 'Hagar the Horrible.' Choose one and see if you can tell what country the characters came from. Locate it on a map or globe. Research the country's history, climate, vegetation and natural resources. What type of homes do the people live in? What form of government do they live under? What is their national sport? Write out your findings."

- Careers

  Objective: To develop insight into various occupations.

  Student directons: "Look for comics that feature professional people (in uniform if they wear one). Research the various occupations and write some brief descriptions for a future discussion on how they help the people in our area."

- Problem Solving

  Objective: To analyze problems in daily living and develop solutions.

  Student directions: "Study the 'Family Circus,' 'Hi and Lois' and 'Peanuts' comic strips in the Sunday paper. Identify problems that characters are having that children you know are also having. Write a paragraph about a comic strip problem, how it was solved and other ways you think it might be solved. Write down a problem you have or know about that you would like to have considered. Post it on our 'Dear Abby' bulletin board for a classmate to respond to. Write an answer to one of the problems you see posted and post your solution under the problem."

5—Funnies Arts

- Dramatics

  Objective: To understand characterization and to perform.

  Student directions: "Prepare a monolog or a pantomime of any cartoon character you like."

- Mobiles

    Objective: To create a mobile that is balanced and pleasing to the eye.

    Student directions: "Cut out several single-frame comics. (Use one theme or character if you like.) Color or paint in the pictures and, laying a string between two frames, paste them back to back. Make several of these cards. Tie them on a coat hanger to make a mobile."

- Coloring Strips

    Objective: To make an inexpensive coloring book.

    Student directions: "Staple together a week or more of the strips of one cartoon from the daily funnies. Color the strips with felt-tip markers, colored pencils or crayons."

- Puppets

    Objective: To develop creativity, cooperation and dramatic action.

    Student directions: "Use a small bag, paper, glue and felt-tip markers to make a puppet of your favorite cartoon character. Get together with a friend who has also made a puppet and plan a show for the class. Be sure to keep your character's commonly known traits in mind."

- Letter Styles

    Objective: To sharpen observation and creative skills.

    Student directions: "Make a display of various lettering styles found in the comic section of your newspaper. Create some of your own."

COMIC BOOKS IN THE CLASSROOM   Mark Cohan

Before we were taught the distinctions between good and bad literature many of us were avid comic book readers. Somehow, the more educated we became, the less we read comics — or, at least, the guiltier we felt if caught leafing through a comic book before buying *Saturday Review* or *National Review*, for example. Rather than reject the use of comics in the classroom, we ought to recognize their strong appeal to young readers. Recognizing this, we might then turn our energies toward using comics to help reach some of our higher instructional goals.

Many students are not used to *thinking* about comics. Perhaps this is the best single justification for their use. To be able to think about that which is taken for granted is an important skill. Sure, comics are fun to read; but what are we reading? Many comic books devote much attention to subjects such as social change, racism, unchecked power, drugs, cultural conflict, and organized crime. Although these issues are often approached through clichés, many social studies teachers know that a well-placed cliché can spark fruitful classroom discussion. A skilled devil's advocate can use comic book clichés to help students learn to think analytically about the world around them. The ability to cope critically with our media environment is a valuable skill. Learning to read a comic book critically — to understand that it is significant as well as fun — may be a step towards coping intelligently with the rest of the media.

The following are some ideas about how comic books can be used in the classroom. Specific examples have been taken from July 1972 and August 1972 issues of comic books.

1.   A teacher can use a comic book and tape recorder to help a student who cannot read or write effectively. Rather than have the student read the comic book story, the teacher can ask him or her to dictate a story to fit the pictures in the book. Dictation is a legitimate form of writing — many best sellers having been written in this manner — and the teacher should make the student aware of this fact. The dictated story should be recorded and saved for future playback. At the same time, the teacher can read the comic book story, as written, and record it. Later, the student can play the taped stories and look at the pictures. Perhaps he or she will begin to "read along" as the recorded version of the original text is played. The teacher can also type a transcript of the student-created story and give it to the student as a gift.

Reprinted with permission of the National Council for the Social Studies from *Social Education* 39 (May 1975): 324-25.

2. A teacher needs three copies of a particular comic book to work with students who can read but who are reluctant to write. Two copies are cut up into their constituent frames (two copies are needed, because the comic is printed on both sides of a page). The third comic remains intact. The teacher puts the cutout frames in a box (a shoe box is fine), and asks the student to create a story out of the pieces. Obviously, there is no "right" or "wrong" solution, the object being the creation of a coherent story. If the student wants to know what the original story was like, the third copy of the comic can be shown to him. This is one way to teach the concept of sequence.

3. Teachers can encourage students to create their own comic books. How about a comic book starring Andrew Carnegie, Woodrow Wilson, Harriet Tubman, Malcolm X, or Gandhi? This activity is well suited to a group of students working together. Some can work on the research and writing, others on the art work, and still others on the editing process. An example of history written in comic book form is *Cuba for Beginners* by Rius (available in paperback).

4. The lead story in a recent *Batman* comic (July 1972) was entitled "Commune of Outcasts" and concerned the efforts of members of a militant street gang, or commune, to save their deteriorating neighborhood from city planners who wish to destroy it and build a superhighway, and from a gang of crooks who wish to turn the neighborhood into their own private preserve. After being ignored at a city planning meeting, the commune plans to stop the bulldozers by means of organized urban guerilla warfare. Batman's mission is to persuade these young street-fighters to win their victory by working within the system. Ultimately, the youth commune defeats City Hall by cleaning up the neighborhood, using psychological warfare, and accepting Batman's help.

This story seems to have been inspired in part by the growing militancy in recent years of urban communities in the face of unsympathetic city bureaucracies. The story can spark a discussion of the issues involved, including the demise of the cities, urban renewal (sometimes called "poor people removal"), and peaceful, as opposed to violent, protest. If students become interested, case studies can be examined, and the resourceful teacher can organize a minicourse in urban problems.

5. Almost every comic book can be used in a discussion of violence in contemporary society. Students can list and categorize the violent incidents in several comic books, and then they may want to discuss questions such as the following: "Would comics sell as well if there were little or no violence in them? Why, or why not?" "Do you think that reading about violence in a comic book might have a bad effect on the character of the reader?" "Should publishers be free to print whatever they wish in their comic books?"

6. Sergeant Fury is the hero of a military comic of the same name. Students may be interested in discussing the specific attributes that seem to make him a hero. Understanding a society's heroes and villains may help us understand something about that society's values.

The above suggestions are merely a few ways in which comic books can be used in the classroom. The possibilities are numerous enough to make a teacher think twice before tearing up a confiscated comic book and throwing it away.

COMPREHENSION THROUGH COMICS

Jill Kaiserman

The compact, humorous stories told within the frames of comic strips found in the daily paper can provide useful and appealing material for reading comprehension activities. Perhaps the following tasks will suggest ways that comic strips might work in your reading program.

- Use comics to check comprehension on several levels. Ask questions calling for factual, inferential or creative thinking.

1. What word does Peppermint Patty use that tells you her teacher is a woman?

2. What kind of test is the class taking? Name two other kinds of test.

3. What does Peppermint Patty mean when she says that this kind of test is "like giving a menu to a starving man"?

- Use comics to study double meanings. The point of many comic strips lies in the use of words with more than one meaning—punning.

1. What did Jughead mean to say?

2. What did Veronica think that Jughead was saying?

3. Veronica's misunderstanding makes the story funny, but often it's important to make meanings very clear. How would you reword what Jughead said so that no one would be likely to misunderstand?

4. List five other double-meaning words that you might use in a comic strip. Try building a funny situation around one of the words.

- Use comics to teach students how to draw conclusions. Look for strips that invite discussion.

1. What do you think might happen next? Why?

2. How would you feel if you were Dagwood?

Reprinted by special permission of *Learning*, The Magazine for Creative Treaching, March 1979. © 1979 by Pitman Learning, Inc., p. 64.

3. What would you do if you were Blondie?

4. Why do you think your chosen action would be the right one to take in this situation?

• Cut-apart comic strips are perfect for students to use to practice sequencing. Make the task more challenging by putting separated frames from three episodes of the same strip into one envelope for sorting out both by story and by sequence within each story.

With comic strips around, reading comprehension activities can provide laughs along with skill development.

III

WHEN?

- coordination of language and art activities

- teaching French vocabulary, expression, grammar, conversation, composition and culture

- during free time and once a week during reading class for club members

- to stimulate and interest students in science

- exploration of current mythic figures

- to display science materials on the bulletin board as an aid for teaching

- English as a foreign language

CARTOON CHARACTERS IN THE LANGUAGE ARTS

Clarence R. Calder, Jr.,
and Julie Carlson McAlpine

Too often teachers unwittingly promote compartmentalization of curriculum areas by teaching them as isolated subjects, failing to interrelate and reinforce one with the other. The language arts premeate all curriculum areas and could serve to coordinate them.

Language and art activities interact well, and both abound in creative potential. Cartooning is an art form which both teachers and students can use with satisfaction in the language arts, and the total curriculum. This is possible, despite many teachers' laments that they "can't draw a straight line," while countless older pupils are afraid to draw, fearing ridicule for not producing conventional forms.

Cartoon drawing is easy and encourages creativity. The cartoonist is striving for a humorous effect so he is delighted when his audience chuckles at his illustrations. Here is an art form which has wide appeal for students; it is easy to execute for the young learner while it is sophisticated enough for the older student.

Study the basic forms for girl and boy cartoon figures. Imagine how you can change the easy-to-sketch lines and shapes to achieve variety in movement, character and decoration.

Illustration 1

That boy could be dressed in a cowboy suit and might be dashing after a steer with lasso swinging. The girl could be attired in mod fashion while swaying to a Top Ten song. Both could use an appropriate caption, bubble of dialogue, or written explanation.

The imaginative teacher will see many uses for cartoon creations in individual and group instruction. Root and suffix cartoon characters could be used to enliven spelling rules for maintaining or dropping final letters. Community helper characters with blurbs brighten social studies.

Cartoons aid in development of number concepts when appropriate numbers of characters are placed with numerals and writing. These clever figures add to a teacher's storytelling, or can be used to check reading comprehension when a child is asked to match several reading selections with cartoon pictures. Teachers could even present cartoon pictures which suggest stories for their budding authors to write. These gay characters when accompanied with words make eyecatching bulletin boards and interest-arresting teaching aids.

Illustration 2

Children might write a comic strip or their own political cartoons after studying current events in social studies. They might sharpen their critical skills by comparing comics with cartoons done by such masters as Munro Leaf. A calendar of months and seasons can be illustrated with cartoon people. Some students might even want to study the art of cartooning and collect samples.

These are just a few ideas for enriching the versatile language arts with cartoon characters. Teachers and children will identify limitless uses for their creations.

Illustration 3

* * *

You may want to turn to two other sources. The first is Techniques and Activities to Stimulate Verbal Learning, by Calder and Antan (New York: Macmillan, 1970). Also read Chapter 10, "Comics and Comic Characters in the Classroom," in Language Arts and Life Patterns by Don M. Wolfe. (New York: The Odyssey Press, 1972, pp. 135-145). This book makes some valuable suggestions related to those by Calder and McAlpine.

* * *

You can make use of these suggestions about cartooning during a study of names. Such a unit is a good one at the beginning of the school year: it emphasizes for children the idea that language is part of the real world, not something entombed in books.

Their own names hold a fascination for children, and both standard "meanings" of names and family reasons for name choices can be researched and discussed.

In addition to personal names, place names can be studied. From one end of the country to the other, residents of unusually-named places are fascinated by the name of their town. What are some different names in your state? Checking a map reveals such unique city names as Red Top (Missouri), Horseheads (New York), Rock Bridge (Illinois), Beanblossom (Indiana), Baresville (Pennsylvania), Bad Axe (Michigan), Thunderbolt (Georgia), and Sleepyeye (Minnesota). Capturing in cartoons the origin, or changes in the town's name can be a challenge for children.

Place name study can be correlated with *social studies*, as one explores city and state names. Tracing the influence of various Indian tribes, the Spanish, or French explorers can also be rewarding. It can correlate with *history*, as for example when one studies the spread of classically named cities across our continent. This classical influence spread as far as Athens (Texas), Attica (Ohio), Corinth (Mississippi), and Rome (Illinois). The widespread use of classical names occurred at a particular stage in our country's history and the reasons for such naming can be investigated. Or such study may be undertaken simply as language arts activity, for instance, when children study city names to find the longest, the shortest, the most or least phonetic, those derived from people's names, or from words for geographical formations.

In studying local or area names, older residents can be interviewed who were present when names were chosen (or changed, as is often the case). This activity, which includes planning questions before and writing reports after the interview, helps increase children's oral language skills.

In studying more remote names, two sources exist. One may simply have children write to the chamber of commerce requesting information. This provides practice in letter writing skills. It is wise to suggest to children that they write to larger cities, avoiding those tiny settlements which may have very picturesque names, but may not have chambers of commerce. Even when so warned, children frequently insist on writing to villages, and we have been delighted by responses from librarians, postmasters, operators of the only store in town, and in one case, a train station master.

In addition to such primary sources, children can go to many books available on this topic. See for example, *Words on the Map*, by Isaac Asimov (Boston: Houghton Mifflin, 1962). There are many of these the teacher can use to augment the primary sources children will consult.

Much of what children learn about place names can be summarized in interesting fashion through cartoons as suggested by Calder and McAlpine.

TEACHING FRENCH WITH THE COMICS   Rufus K. Marsh

Pedagogical literature on comics is abundant and, like the critical literature on the subject, most of it is being written in Europe, particularly in France, where the instructional use of comics (*la bande dessinée or BD*) is widely accepted.[1] One advanced, theoretical approach stresses the uniqueness of the genre and what it can reveal of French culture, when used in literature and civilization courses.[2] Other writers have recently conceived oral and written exercises and tests for use mainly in elementary French.[3] Their proposed exercises, like the language texts now incorporating comics, are based on comics that were specifically designed for instructional purposes. A notable exception is Bernard Marsadié and Roland Saint-Péron, "Exploitation pédagogique des bandes dessinées de la presse des jeunes Français."[4] One shortcoming of this literature on teaching French via the comics is that, though it appears to be directed toward elementary and intermediate secondary school teaching, it makes at best only approximate indications of age and academic level. Moreover, no critical evaluation, no student feedback is offered on the effectiveness of the use of comics in the classroom. The present study attempts to complement this theoretical literature by demonstrating the use of selected popular French language comics in intermediate college language instruction. It describes four major purposes for which different comics were found useful: (1) vocabulary and expressions; (2) grammar; (3) conversation and composition; (4) culture; also pronunciation, intonation and listening comprehension. It discusses the results of a survey of student opinion on major aspects of the instructional use of comics.

By means of spirit-master handouts and overhead and slide projectors, I was able to introduce the world of the *bande dessinée*, with its lively use of language, visually reinforced, into the classroom at a minimal cost. Use of the comics was limited to the classroom. I assigned no outside work in them. I used the comics as a supplement to reading and grammar texts,[5] approximately once a week for twenty minutes, during the semester. Starting with French adaptations of American comic strips, *Me faire ça à moi, Charlie Brown* (Holt, 1974), then *Le Journal de Mickey: Mickey Parade* (Edi-Monde, 1972), I proceeded to use excerpts from French comic books with American or British themes: *Calamity Jane* (Dupuis, 1970), a *Lucky Luke* title, followed by *Tintin en Amérique* (Casterman, 1974), and finally *Astérix chez les Bretons* (Dargaud, 1966).

Reprinted with permission of the author and The American Association of Teachers of French from *French Review* 51 (May 1978): 777-85.

I. An Early Experiment

I chose to begin with *Charlie Brown* because of its simplicity, clarity and wide appeal. My intention was to exploit the familiar representation of human dilemmas and conflicts for general purposes of discussion and language study. For example, in *Me faire ça à moi, Charlie Brown*, an optimistic Linus learns there is to be a true-false test and conceives a system for passing it (p. 8). Next we see him as he returns home, dejected, and explains to Lucy that he has failed. She replies that it was because he had not studied: "Tu as échoué parce que tu n'as pas étudié." Linus retorts no, it was because he had started with a *faux* instead of a *vrai*, implying that his system would have proven sound if only he had started the other way around. Lucy is disgusted: "Ah, misère!" (p. 9).

I began by describing the situation simply and briefly in French, at the same time explaining new vocabulary and expressions. I did this as an exercise in listening comprehension before students saw the strips. This oral introduction also prepared students for the discussion which followed the reading of the strips. I then distributed spirit-master copies of all four strips (sixteen frames). Two students took parts and read the dialogue of the last two strips. Since the dialogue is short it also allowed a number of students to work on pronunciation and especially intonation of a variety of affirmative, interrogative, and exclamatory utterances. After dealing with preliminary questions from students, I asked them questions of fact and interpretation, proceeding from the simple to the complex and reviewing previously-studied vocabulary and syntax:

Comment s'appelle la jeune fille?

Comment s'appelle le garçon?

Où se trouvent-ils? (A la maison; dans la salle de séjour; devant la télévision …)

Quel est l'état d'esprit de Linus? Pourquoi?

Quelle est l'attitude de Lucy? Expliquez.

Pourquoi Linus est-il assis devant la télé?

Pourquoi Lucy reste-t-elle toujours debout?

I called on individual students, or the class as a whole, to present orally simple and compound sentences in anticipation of written summaries to follow. Since the action of these strips is straightforward, I asked questions and held discussion prior to our intensive study of the language of the strips. The excerpts from the French comics presented more difficult vocabulary and more complex sentences, and students' linguistic means seemed inadequate at the outset. I therefore reversed the procedure and had language study precede discussion of contents. As a final exercise, following thorough study of a sketch, I would, in subsequent use of comics, call for written summaries to reinforce the oral work. A "write-up," even as short as five minutes, containing only one or two sentences from each student, also gave me some indication of the effectiveness of the medium and permitted me to weigh students' reactions to the sketch as a guide to further use of comics. While I used *Charlie Brown* experimentally for a variety of purposes of language instruction, I later discovered that different comics lend themselves best to one or more major instructional uses and not to all on on an equal basis.

II. Instructional Uses

1. Vocabulary and Expressions

The same selection from *Me faire ça à moi, Charlie Brown* contains a variety of useful and lively words and expressions: "épreuve," "échouer," "erreur de calcul," "au lieu de," "Ça a marché?" "tais-toi," "Qu'est-ce qui s'est passé?" "Ça te servira de leçon!" For certain expressions I devised substitution drills, such as replacing "cette épreuve" with, for example, "cet examen," "cette interview," "ce match de basket," in the following: LUCY. — Alors, cette épreuve, ça a marché? LINUS. — Ah, tais-toi ... un vrai désastre!" At my invitation students continued with substitutions of their own. "Ça te servira de leçon" was approximated to similar English expressions: "Serves you right," "Let that be a lesson to you," and along with "tais-toi" was used for a review of French *tutoiement*.

Mickey presents no less varied and lively use of language than *Charlie Brown*. In a strip taken from *Le Journal de Mickey: Mickey Parade*, Goofy, driving on a country road, tells his passenger Mickey of his surprise at escaping a traffic jam, especially as the car's brakes do not work. He tries to calm Mickey's nerves, saying that brakes are not needed, since he knows the road by heart. At the foot of a hill, however, the car splashes into a river. The bridge that Goofy says was there the week before is no longer in place. Vocabulary and expressions include: "embouteillage," "énervant," "freins," "pont coupé," "Hein? Quoi?" "Ne t'inquiète pas surtout, nous n'aurons pas à nous en servir!" "Je connais la route par coeur!" "Sapristi!" (p. 1).

Calamity Jane presents abundant material for contrastive vocabulary study. When the heroine rescues Lucky Luke from a band of Apaches, she calls him "pied tendre" (tenderfoot) for separating himself from his "artillerie," and "corne verte" (greenhorn). At his invitation to share his meal, she replies, "Avec plaisir. Je n'ai jamais su faire la cuisine," but she refuses his offer of a cigarette: "Je ne fume pas. Je chique" (pp. 4-5). Comic books such as *Lucky Luke, Tintin* and *Astérix* present a variety of vocabulary and expressions that can be studied more systematically than in the simpler strips. For this purpose, in more extensive future use of comics, I would group words and expressions within categories, e.g., cowboys and Indians, cops and robbers, eating and drinking, fighting.

2. Grammar

As a supplement to our work in the grammar text, I found certain scenes in the comics that visually and dramatically reinforced the use of moods and tenses. In the strips taken from *Me faire ça à moi, Charlie Brown*, for example, students composed compound sentences with *si* and *parce que* using models found in the dialogue, such as "Si j'avais commencé par un 'faux' au lieu d'un 'vrai.' " I asked them to complete and simplify this sentence using *réussir, ne pas échouer, avoir, recevoir un A, une bonne note*, etc., in appropriate tenses and with variations on the personal pronoun. We exploited Lucy's moral indignation: "Tu as échoué parce que tu n'as pas étudié" (p. 9), and in *Le Journal de Mickey: Mickey Parade* a lively model for indirect discourse was "Je te jure qu'il [le pont] était encore là la semaine dernière" (p. 1).

In the opening scene of *Calamity Jane*, Lucky Luke, riding Jolly Jumper, arrives at a river's edge and decides to bathe. His horse modestly turns his head the other way. Finding himself in midstream, Lucky hears the war cry of an approaching party of Apaches, "ADADA! ADADA! ADADA!" As he starts to swim for shore he says to himself, "Il faut que je reprenne mon revolver!" (p. 3). With this equivalent of "Gotta get my gun!" the situation becomes more familiar to American readers, following the exaggerated modesty of his talking horse or the unusual Apache war cry, which, like the name Lucky Luke, is good for a brief phonetic exercise. The sudden intensity of the situation, which I exploited by projecting a slide close-up, lends itself to a simple review of the subjunctive: "Que faut-il que Lucky Luke fasse?" "Il faut qu'il reprenne son revolver ... sorte de l'eau ... se défende ... se batte, etc." In our collective oral summary of this scene, I emphasized the use of the *passé composé* and the *imparfait* to distinguish between action and description, or, in the case of Lucky Luke surprised in his bath, interrupted action in the past. Having perceived this distinction visually, a student would write, for example: "Lucky se baignait dans une rivière quand les Apaches sont arrivés." In *Tintin en Amérique* a gangster who is about to plunge Tintin into the grinding mechanism of a canned food factory says ironically: "Si vous tombiez là-dedans, vous seriez aussitôt broyé par les énormes malaxeurs que vous voyez là, sous vos pieds!" Tintin replies, "Ce ne serait pas drôle!" (p. 53). I projected a slide close-up of this panel, again using the visual intensity of the situation for the purpose of tense study and drill.

3. Composition and Conversation

In my use of the comics students answered orally specific questions which I asked on the contents, as in the case of *Me faire ça à moi, Charlie Brown*. They also made oral summaries, as in the case of the excerpt from *Calamity Jane*. The spontaneity and liveliness of dialogue in the comics can be exploited further. In future use of comics, I would have small group discussions take place between two or more students, after which I would call upon a discussant from each group to report briefly on its observations. This activity would be especially useful in the case of strips taken from *Me faire ça à moi, Charlie Brown*, with its psychological conflicts, and the excerpts from *Calamity Jane* and *Tintin en Amérique*, with their cultural and satirical content. Interviews and skits would be appropriate in the case of Lucy's and Linus's confrontation, Mickey's accident, Tintin's narrow escape, and Lucky Luke's embarrassment.

In my use of comics I sometimes called for a written summary following discussion and language study, as in the case of *Calamity Jane* with its colorful action, personality, and dialogue. This served essentially to reinforce expressions and constructions used in the preceding oral work. With simpler strips such as *Charlie Brown* I blanked out the dialogue by means of a photocopier and liquid paper. I selected some strips which emphasized dialogue, for example, Lucy courting Schroeder at the piano, others emphasizing action. Students often supplied convincing, imaginative dialogues, which I read to the class as an exercise in listening comprehension.

4.   Culture

Even in French, American comics such as *Charlie Brown* and *Mickey* present situations and behavior with which an American reader can readily identify, whereas *Calamity Jane* and *Tintin en Amérique* reveal a different, less familiar perception of American characteristics. In fact, the exaggeration of American manners and morals in these French comics, and of British behavior in *Astérix chez les Bretons*, leaves students confused at first. A second, closer reading is necessary in order to discover that this exaggeration indirectly conveys a sense of French culture. For example, the humorous caricature of American puritanical modesty in Lucky Luke and his horse suggests, by implication, a French acceptance of natural bodily functions.

In *Tintin en Amérique* my students and I explored an excerpt set in Chicago. In it, the mob boss, with his large forehead, completely bald, impeccably dressed, appears as a sinister mastermind with influence at all levels of society, a caricature of Vautrin. Tom, his contact at Slift canned meat factory, who has orders to rub out Tintin while ostensibly giving him a tour of the works, is depicted as a clever, cynical opportunist. Both gangsters operate in indirect, devious ways, rather than by direct force as in the usual American stereotypes. The assembly-line canning process is presented as an instantaneous transformation from cow (dogs and cats are mentioned but not shown) into corned beef. Here the satire reveals a French fascination with automated assembly-line techniques. What saves Tintin when Tom presses the secret button, causing him to plunge into the mixing vat, is that workers have called a strike and stopped the machines. Taken unawares, Tom puts on a categorical air as if berating children. The workers respond with an attitude of stubborn resistance. This clearly polarized, formal behavior is evidently less characteristic of American than of French relations between superiors and subordinates (pp. 53-54).

Toward the end of the semester I used the opening pages of *Astérix chez les Bretons* to make a brief introduction to certain representations of British behavior. For example, on sighting the Roman fleet, one Breton says, "Bonté gracieuse! Ce spectacle est surprenant!" The other replies, "Il est, n'est-il pas?" My students did not all immediately recognize such utterances as anglicized French. War with the Romans is constantly interrupted for tea or the weekend. Jolitorax, raised in the Cambridge tribe, rows expertly across the Channel in search of his cousin Astérix. Upon asking to shake hands with Obélix, he says, "Secouons-nous les mains!" Jolitorax is pounded mercilessly, to which he reacts in sportsmanlike admiration of Obélix's strength, "Splendide! Splendide!" (pp. 6-8).

The cultural content in *Tintin en Amérizue* and *Astérix chez les Bretons* is further enriched by the confrontation of nationalities which these comics present. *Calamity Jane*, whose main characters are represented as having an identical national, even regional, background, is less evidently rich in this respect, although French manners and morals are implied, as in the caricature of American puritanical modesty. However, the satire enhances positive characteristics of American fictional heroes, toughness and purity. There is no overt social criticism of the U.S. to which students may object, as in *Tintin en Amérique*. Nor are there less familiar, non-U.S. stereotypes, as in *Astérix chez les Bretons. Calamity Jane* and other *Lucky Luke* titles may thus help overcome some of the problems of initiating students to French culture by allowing the instructor to proceed gradually from the familiar to the less familiar. Comics such as *Tintin en Amérique* and *Astérix chez les Bretons* are best used with students who are already somewhat conversant with French culture.[6]

III. Student Feedback

In my survey of student opinion the class as a whole found the comics a far more effective inducement to speak French than the reader. Students expressly favored the everyday, casual quality of speech used in the comics. As one student said: "As for idioms and vocabulary, in comic strips it is less formal, like a conversation between you and me, which is more or less what the kids want to know rather than the traditional 'Parlez-vous français?' or 'Comment allez-vous?' I personally would rather know how to say things more comparable to the way I talk to my peers. Also you have a chance of running into better idioms in more common language." Furthermore, the class considered vocabulary and idioms to be more effectively presented than grammar via the comics. This is understandable at first, since concrete words and expressions are immediately identifiable in the visual medium, while systematic grammatical structure seems abstract and far removed from it. One student tried to express this distinction: "They [the comics] ... only can provide some examples of the use of grammar." He or she may thus be assuming that students have to learn the total grammatical apparatus of the language. This is, however, a fruitless if not impossible task for most students in their third semester of a language. Rather, an instructor chooses to emphasize certain key points of grammar.

One that I chose to emphasize was the use of tenses and moods. For this purpose the comics were as useful as for teaching vocabulary and expressions. The visual reinforcement was perhaps less immediate, but no less strong, in my use of Lucky Luke's predicament to demonstrate a basic distinction between the *imparfait* and the *passé composé*, and in certain scenes of dramatic intensity, e.g., "Il faut que je reprenne mon revolver" (*Calamity Jane*, p. 3); "Si vous tombiez là-dedans" (*Tintin en Amérique*, p. 53). As another student put it: "The comics can be more effective as a way of learning vocabulary and grammar because they have less material, which can be covered more thoroughly." By "less material" this student may be referring to the notion of the single picture that is worth a thousand words. However, in the comics that I used the pictures do not replace the need for words. There are both pictures and words. The printed and visual contexts mutually explain each other, thus supplying the instructor with a ready-made tool for emphasizing elements of language that he chooses to present.

The class rated the comics nearly equal with the reader as a means of understanding French culture. However, students indicated a preference for the

"American strips." *Charlie Brown* was the favorite, followed by *Lucky Luke, Mickey, Tintin,* and *Astérix.* Two students tried to explain: "*Charlie Brown* illustrated the grammar most clearly and simply. *Astérix* cannot really be compared to the others since it is more culture than language"; "I found that I liked the more American strips better, like *Charlie Brown* and *Lucky Luke.*" One reason for their preference is that *Charlie Brown* is the simplest and clearest strip and technically the easiest to present with visual media. *Astérix* is the most detailed and difficult to present. The rest are in between. Another reason has to do with cultural and satirical content, which requires careful introduction, close reading, and some knowledge of French civilization on the part of students.

The class preferred the slides to the overhead transparencies. As a number of student explained, this was essentially a preference for color over black and white. However, one student expressly preferred the overhead for providing "a very crisp, clear picture and a communal feeling in the class." The instructor, on the other hand, must also be careful to maintain what could be called a "communicative feeling." For exposing students to a bright, familiar image in a darkened classroom has distinct limitations and distinct advantages. Whether on a screen or on a handout, the combined visual and anecdotal intensity of the comic strip runs the risk of drawing all attention to it, at the expense of the linguistic and cultural elements the instructor may choose to emphasize. With this in mind the instructor should be aware of the right moment to turn off the machine and begin oral work, or to have the handouts set aside and assign written summaries. Otherwise, as far as language teaching is concerned, the strength of the strips may become their weakness. It is along these lines that the specific opportunities and problems of the instructional use of comics remain to be explored further.

It is already evident to me, however, that the power of reinforcement of the *bande dessinée* is not limited to vocabulary and grammar. Like the visit of certain French natives to the classroom, it conveys a sense of the authenticity of French language and culture. Students experience the adaptation of French to a familiar, popular medium, one that confirms immediately the liveliness of the language and, upon further analysis, the distinctive character of French culture. The verification of these qualities, as afforded by the *bande dessinée,* makes it a powerful additional tool of language instruction.

Notes

[1]James W. Brown discusses the work of European pedagogical scholars in "Comics in the Foreign Language Classroom: Pedagogical Perspectives," *FLA,* 10 (Feb. 1977), 18-25, and urges foreign language teachers in North America "to develop more rigorous methodologies of comics" (p. 25). To his useful selective bibliography, one may add Pierre Fresnault-Deruelle, *Récits et discours par la bande: essais sur les comics* (Paris: Hachette, 1977); *Magazine littéraire,* no. 95 (Dec. 1974), pp. 8-37; Georges Pernin, *Un Monde étrange: la bande dessinée* (Paris: Clédor, 1974); Christopher Pinet, "Myths and Stereotypes in *Astérix le*

Gaulois," in *Contemporary French Civilization*, I (Spring 1977) rpt., *The Canadian Modern Language Review*, 34 (Jan. 1978).

[2]See the works of Fresnault-Deruelle, esp. *Dessins et bulles: la bande dessinée comme moyen d'expression* (Paris: Bordas, 1972), its accompanying *Travaux dirigés*, and "La Langue des bandes dessinées et leur contenu culturel," *FMonde*, no. 98 (July-Aug. 1973), pp. 14-19.

[3]Georges Rollet, "Des bandes dessinées ... pourquoi?" *FMonde*, no. 107 (Sept. 1974), pp. 14-18, proposes, for example: having students express orally their first brief impressions of a strip; interviews between two students, one of whom identifies with a character in a strip; skits based on a strip; creating compound sentences expressing causal or temporal relations between frames. He suggests methods of testing with strips, e.g., finding the proper sequence of sentences given in random order, each of which describes a single frame; also questions and compositions. His exercises and tests are intended for use with his textbook, *Parler et écrire avec la bande dessinée* (Hachette, n.d.). Jacques Verdol, "Art et manière d'utiliser une B.D. de *Feu vert*," *FMonde*, no. 122 (July 1976), pp. 33-34, proposes exercises similar to Rollet's and adds, notably, analysis of characters' attitudes and various games, esp. with blanked-out balloons. *Feu vert* is a text of instructional comics also published by Hachette.

[4]*FMonde*, no. 98 (July-Aug. 1973), pp. 25-32. These writers propose exercises in oral and written expression and in reading comprehension, including: transcribing the contents of the balloons in indirect discourse; reading aloud for intonation; describing the contents of a frame hidden from view; imagining the thoughts of characters in a "silent" frame; relating the sketch from the point of view of a character; confronting a written account of the sketch ("code écrit") with a description of its purely visual elements ("code iconographique"); replacing the written contents sequentially when balloons are blanked and their contents given out of sequence; creating dialogue for blanked-out balloons, perhaps assigning roles.

[5]Our grammar text was *En bonne forme* (Heath, 1973), in which we concentrated on the use of tenses. The reader was primarily *Variété du conte français* (Holt, 1972), in which we read stories by Mérimée, Zola, Maupassant, Aymé, Courteline, Apollinaire. At the end of the semester we also read Anouilh's *Antigone* (Didier, 1964). All class discussions and oral exercises took place in French.

[6]For a discussion of cultural content in *Astérix* and its possible use in a civilization course, see Pinet, "Myths." For prices of French comics available in the U.S., consult foreign language catalogues, e.g., Continental Book Co., 11-03 46th Av., Long Island City, NY 11101; Gessler Publ. Co., 220 E. 23d St., NY 10010, and bookstores, e.g., Librairie de France, 610 5th Av., NY 10020; Midwest European Publications, 3229 W. Clark St., Chicago, IL 60657; European Book Co., 925 Larkin St., San Francisco, CA 94108. *Charlie Brown*, published by Holt, seems to be the least expensive and most readily available in the U.S.

Appendix: Comics and Visual Instructional Media

Comics included in the present study are available for purchase in the United States (see n. 6). However, handouts allow individual students to have personal copies of single strips or excerpts from a variety of titles. Black and white comics such as *Charlie Brown* and *Mickey* yield clear spirit-master duplicates. Comics in color, *Lucky Luke, Tintin,* and especially *Astérix* with its fine detail and small print, require more accurate and expensive techniques, such as photocopy. With either duplicates or the comic book itself in hand, students can take parts in reading the dialogue and concentrate on intensive language study. Projected images, which draw the collective attention of the class, are appropriately used to introduce a comic, to dramatize a specific frame or balloon, or for review. A slide or transparency close-up of a single well-chosen frame, following projection of the full page, has a startling effect in emphasizing the use of language in a visually dramatic situation. Close-ups, especially transparency close-ups, are the best means of projecting *Astérix* or densely rich scenes in other comics. However, without making enlargements, the instructor can achieve similar effects with the overhead projector by means of masking techniques. While overhead transparency images are normally limited to black and white or uniform background colors, slides reproduce the various colors of the original. A zoom slide projector lens is recommended, mainly in order to overcome problems involved in projecting the printed word. For further advice on the use of visuals, consult persons in Instructional Media. Some simple, imaginative uses of visuals are described in Ed Minor and Harvey R. Frye, *Techniques for Producing Visual Instructional Media*, 2nd ed. (New York: McGraw-Hill, 1977). Current prices and descriptions of equipment are given annually in *The Audio-Visual Equipment Directory* (Fairfax, Va.: National Audio-Visual Assn., Inc.).

COMIC BOOK CLUB

Ann Carlyle

We're a country of joiners, with organizations for every interest. If your kids are hooked on comic books, you might suggest a comic book club—for the greater enjoyment of comics and integration of comics into many phases of the curriculum.

Club members are responsible for starting a club library of comics. If each member is able to bring in three to five comic books, that should get the club off to a good start.

Members may read comics during their free time, and one day a week comics become the regular fare for their reading classes. One enjoyable way of using comics is for each reader to take a character and read that character's speech balloons aloud, following along in the story sequence. (The comic-book format is perfect for this sort of "readers theater" production.)

Each member of the comic book club is required to complete one special project a week to retain membership. Here is a list of suggestions:

1. Make a poster for your favorite character. (An opaque projector can be useful here.)

2. Write 10 facts about your favorite character.

3. Pretend your character is in our class. Write about one day's happenings. Include conversations with your character.

4. Write a list of 10 things you might find in the top drawer of your favorite character's dresser.

5. Find out when your character was first drawn. Find out about the artist and creator.

6. Trace a page out of a comic book, but leave off the words in the speech balloons. Prepare the page for duplication on a ditto master. See what other students put in the balloons. (Make your own version of what goes in the balloons too.)

7. Make hand puppets or papier-mâché figures that are comic characters.

Reprinted by permission of the author and *Learning*, The Magazine for Creative Teaching, April 1978. © 1978 by Pitman Learning, Inc., p. 48.

8. Make a costume for one of the figures you made in Project 7.

9. Arrange an unlikely meeting of two characters from different comics, and write their conversation.

10. Create a family tree or name the relatives of some comic character.

11. Write a letter to the editor of a comic book. Ask four questions.

12. Make a comic-character wordsearch maze for fellow club members to solve.

13. Make a list of 10 to 15 exclamations and sound-effect words used in comics.

14. Make a glossary of symbols in comics.

15. Find and list 10 words that are new to you. Find and write their definitions.

16. Survey other members on their favorite characters. Graph the data.

17. Survey other members on the number of comics they have. Graph the data.

18. Graph the number of times something violent happens in the first 10 pages of several different comic books. (Count kicks, shoves, punches, etc.)

19. List commercial products that use comic characters in advertising.

20. Decorate a notebook or other useful item with comic characters.

This is a club that should thrive even without a president, regular meetings or a secret handshake—but such elements can be added if the comic club membership stops reading long enough to vote.

COMICS: NO-NONSENSE CLASSROOM AIDS

Charles E. Carraher

Is there any reason why Superman, or Atomic Bunny for that matter, shouldn't come to the rescue of beleagured science teachers, especially those interested in stimulating their students toward an interest in science?

Whatever your view of comic books, they sell briskly, especially to high school and college students. I have found that I can make good use of them in the science classroom, particularly for introducing new topics. Since I am a chemistry teacher, most of my examples will pertain to that field. But teachers of other sciences should find equally interesting material in the comics.

At appropriate points in a lecture, I flash color slides of comic book covers on a screen. For example, Plastic Man doing his contortions is used to introduce polymer, plastic, or rubber chemistry. There seems to be a character to meet my every need: For introductory lectures on problem solving and equation balancing, I call on Molecule Man and Mole Man. Lectures on metals are enlivened with slides of Iron Man, Quicksilver, Silver Surfer, Cobalt Man, the Metal Men (Tin, Mercury, Gold and Iron), and Golden Arrow. For nuclear and other forms of energy and the atom there are E-Man, Doctor Solar, Atom Smasher, The Atom, Captain Atom, and the Atomic Knights; for water chemistry, the Sea Devils, Aqualad and Aquaman; for lectures dealing with chemical reactions, the Sandman, Rusty (Rust), and (for sheer number of elements and compounds mentioned) Metamorpho; for organic chemistry there are Coal Man, Carbon Copy Man, and Sugarfoot; for alloys there is Superman — "Man of Steel," and Dr. Savage — "Man of Bronze." Covers emphasizing ecology are also numerous.[1]

Comic books and comic book characters can also be used in tests and homework assignments. For example, imagine The Atom has been captured by diabolical Dr. Doom and placed in a room containing radioactive material. Can students name four principles of radiation protection The Atom should utilize for safety? Ask students to read a particular comic and to comment on the accuracy of the science it contains, or ask them to discuss attitudes toward science displayed by various characters.

Many students are unable to compose even simple sentences or to express themselves in writing. I ask them to invent or utilize an already known hero and to write a short story about the hero's exploits, incorporating scientific concepts learned in class. Some students who enjoy design make bulletin board displays.

Reprinted with permission from *The Science Teacher* (November 1975), published by the National Science Teachers Association.

One of the best dialogues about the mistaken overemphasis of science is found in issue #2 of "Captain Venture and the Land Beneath the Sea," where a "mad" scientist yells to Captain Venture that "Science is All, Science Conquers All, it has All the answers to every problem." Comic books make excellent motivators. And, by establishing a common interest, permit students to identify more with the teacher—a positive move, I believe.

Note

[1]Many suitable comics are currently published and on sale. Most cities have at least one dealer in used comics—easily located in the Yellow Pages under "Books." There is also a *Readers Buyers Guide* (Dynapubs., R.R. 1, Box 297, East Moline, IL 61244); $3/year for 24 issues of comics ads. Most of us are shocked at the current prices of comics we discarded in our youth. The first issue of *Action*, in good condition, can bring over $4,000.

ORIGINS: WHERE DID I COME FROM?
WHERE AM I GOING?

Herb Kohl

One day I read my class the following Seneca tale: "A man who was a crow was traveling. He didn't know where he had come from or which way he was going. As he moved along he kept thinking: 'How did I come to be alive? Where did I come from? Where am I going?' "

One student responded immediately. "You know I've had the same questions. Did the Seneca Indians worry about those things, too?"

I used this unexpected response to talk about the concern people, from as early as we can trace, have always had about their origins and their futures. "Where did I come from?" "How did I get to be the way I am?"

These questions seem to be as old as language. Every mythology begins with accounts of origins—how the earth came to be, why there is order instead of chaos, how people were created, why people walk upright, how language was made, how food and shelter originated. Here, for example. is an Eskimo tale of origins:

"There was once a girl who lived in the open desert of white snow. One day she went in a boat with a man who suddenly threw her into the sea. When she tried to hold on to the side of the boat, he cut her fingers off so that the boat would not turn over. She sank to the bottom of the sea where she made her home inside a large bubble. Here she became the mother of all life in the sea. The fingers she had lost grew into seals and walrus. And the people of this frozen land now had food to eat. Now they had skins for warmth. Now they had oil for the long nights of winter."

In this tale the mother of all life in the sea is a person who has been harmed. But the fingers she lost became food for people. The destructive can become creative. This simple story embodies a way of looking at people and their relationship to nature—a unity of life to be respected.

Contemporary Myths

Mythic figures aren't only from the past. The lives of many contemporary characters encountered on TV and in the theater also represent versions of how things began and why they are as they are. For many young people, the most powerful mythic figures created in our time are those in comic books. The stories of the origins of comic-book superheroes reveal aspects of our culture just as the Eskimo myth displayed some values of that culture.

In discussing and reading about origins, students are fascinated when some of the contemporary superheroes they know so well from comic books and TV are included. It gives them a sense that what they know and care about is important and can be the subject of serious analysis.

I remember discussing Superman with my class once. He is an alien born on the planet Krypton, which was destroyed in an atomic holocaust. He was saved by his parents and sent to Earth. He is stronger and purer than the rest of us. The alien Superman becomes our hero and protector. He presents human frailties only through Clark Kent, his earthly identity. The savior of Metropolis, a mythic city, is not one of us. The students quickly picked up on what may be the central theme of the Superman myth—that people can't save themselves but need help from another world.

Wonder Woman is another superhero that is interesting to consider in class. Born on Paradise Isle where no man lives, her original name was Princess Diana. During the Second World War, Steve Trevor, an American pilot, crashed on Paradise Isle. He and Princess Diana fell in love. Eventually she had to choose between love and loyalty to the Amazons, her people. One of the early Wonder Woman comics describes her choice: "And so, Princess Diana, the Wonder Woman, giving up her heritage and her right to eternal life, leaves Paradise Isle to take the man she loves back to America—the land she learns to love and protect, and adopts as her own!"

Again an alien comes to rescue us. This time her motive is love. For Superman the motive was to prevent Earth from destroying itself the way Krypton did.

The Hulk is a more recent superhero. The story of his origin is the reverse of that of Wonder Woman and Superman. The Hulk was born a human, Bruce Banner, who became a famous nuclear physicist. In experimenting with physical forces beyond his control, Dr. Banner found himself transformed into the Hulk, a superhuman though subintelligent force. Bruce Banner and the Hulk are a contemporary version of Dr. Jekyll and Mr. Hyde. It is never clear, however, whether the Hulk is a positive or negative force. The problem posed by the Hulk is whether science is positive or negative when it gets the upper hand.

Myth Making

Mythology is open-ended. We can all create our own villains and superheroes. One way to get your students involved in writing is to have them create their own characters and make their own comic books. Students' first efforts will usually be direct imitations of comics they have read or stories they have seen on TV. However, thinking about the origins of their creations can help students clarify and develop them. The tales of their beginnings can be a springboard for stories that don't depend on stereotypes drawn from comics and TV.

Where did these new mythic figures come from? How did they get their powers? Do they have relatives? Are there limits to their powers? Do they need to eat or rest or be fueled? Do they have any connections with their old lives? All these questions help create in-depth characters and give a reality to the imaginary lives created by your students.

Young children enjoy making up wild explanations for things whenever they have the chance. Here are a few examples of origins themes that can lead to interesting writing:

1. "Why are ... ?" tales. Why are owls creatures of the night? Why are there stars? Why are there so many animals? Why are there night and day? Why does it rain?

2. "Why is there ... ?" tales. Why is there hair? Why is there love? Hate? Laughter? Tears?

3. "Why do ... ?" tales. Why do people live in the air and fish in the water? Why do animals let themselves be tamed by people? Why do people stop growing? Why do living things die?

4. "Why don't ... ?" stories. Why don't animals talk? Why don't people fly? Why don't trees walk? Why don't stones cry?

Considering our own origins, those of superheroes and even the everyday things that are often taken for granted has appealed to my students—no matter what their age. It gets them thinking, reasoning, imagining and writing.

SCIENCE CARTOONS

Maurice K. Schiffman

Most children enjoy cartoons and they are readily available in **Current Science,** other science magazines, and the local papers. They make a good format for a bulletin board. I divide a large bulletin board in the science classroom or in the hall into several categories.

The greater the number of subjects, the easier it is to find cartoons that fit the subject headings. Students bring cartoons to class, and after discussion decide under which science subject each cartoon is to be placed. The student who submitted the cartoon has the privilege of fastening it to the board. The cartoon categories need not be as general as shown. The subject may be divisions or units of any one science as earth, physical, or biological.

Two objectives are achieved with this activity: the students read more science material in order to find cartoons and have an introduction to classification (taxonomy), as the class decides which basic or applied science is applicable to a cartoon on the bulletin board.

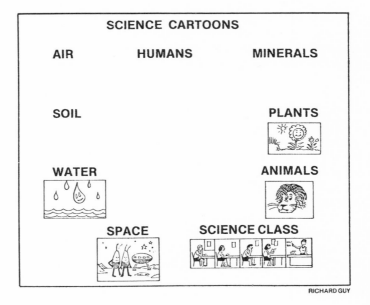

Reproduced with permission from *Science and Children*, November/December 1977. Copyright © 1977 by the National Science Teachers Association, 1742 Connecticut Avenue, NW, Washington, DC 20009.

COMIC STRIPS IN THE TEACHING
OF ENGLISH AS A FOREIGN LANGUAGE

Robert J. Elkins
and Christian Brüggemann

Language teachers as well as other teachers are constantly searching for new methods and techniques to improve their teaching effectiveness. Often the materials which could assist them in their task are flaunted in their faces without teachers being aware of them. Such potential material exists in newspaper comic strips and cartoons. Not only would the efficient use of these forms of mass media lend an enjoyable variety to the classroom, but also their introduction would offer the students an inside look into American life and thought, the Americans' preoccupations, their idiosyncracies and some of their characteristics, all in concentrated or capsule form.

Comics, although known throughout the world, do not enjoy the popularity in other countries to the extent they do in the United States. Bond, in *An Introduction to Journalism*, states that, "The latest published statistics proclaim that 82 per cent of men readers and 78 per cent of women readers daily devour the comics."[1] Scarcely any American paper, no matter how small, devotes less than one page daily to comic strips. Sundays, one finds 4 to 12 full pages of comics in color. Of the larger papers, only the New York "Times" includes no comics.

Should not and could not language teachers take advantage of this form of mass media to increase interest and appeal in their classes? An example of the comic strip's effectiveness and potential value to teaching is pointed out by Alvin Silverman in *The American Newspaper*, "So many people in America read the comics that, during World War II, the strips were used to teach men and women in the armed forces."[2] Their major use at that time was to help servicemen learn foreign languages. When American comics were introduced into Bolivia and reached the areas where the Indian population was largely illiterate, there was an increase in the desire to learn to read. The reason was found to be that the Indians wished to know what such characters as "Mutt" and "Jeff" were saying.[3] Businessmen have also recognized the potential of comics and often develop their advertisements in the format of the comic strip.[4]

For the purposes of this paper, the comic strip will be separated from the older version, the cartoon, and subsequently dealt with exclusively. A number of various definitions have been presented for the comic strip. Silverman says, "a comic strip is a series of pictures in a related order. A single picture is called a cartoon."[5] Bond considers the cartoon to be a "pictured editorial."[6] The American College Dictionary states that a cartoon is "1) a sketch or drawing as in

ERIC Document ED 056 591, February 1971.

a newspaper or periodical, symbolizing or caricaturing some subject or person of current interest, in an exaggerated way. 2) ... 3) a comic strip."[7]

The word cartoon does not inherently imply humour although Spencer states that it does. "The very word cartoon implies humor, ..."[8] Yet the topics dealt with are not particularly or necessarily humourous. Spencer continues by stating, "the humor varies; some grim, some pathetic, some sad, some ironic, some bitter — but all portraying a measure of truth."[9] Comic on the other hand connotes "humour" or "funny" with the result that the comics are often referred to as "the funnies" or the "funny papers." Comic strips are not all humourous but often handle topics dealing with crime, adventure, or mystery.

In this paper, cartoon is used to describe a single panel based upon a contemporary event or a caricature of a current public figure and dependent upon the reader's knowledge of current facts and events. These cartoons, basically political and generally found on the editorial page, will not be dealt with since students must first be given current background information and such information could not be prepared by a textbook writer or teacher beforehand. Once the event is in the realm of the past, the value usually diminishes or becomes non-existent. The writers of this paper do recognize the value of cartoons, however, and recommend that they be utilized whenever applicable. Their value has been demonstrated by their recognition by the Pulitzer Prize Committee which has yearly awarded the "Pulitzer Prize for Editorial Cartooning" since 1922.[10] For the classroom, the comic or comic strip should prove more practical and can be prepared for in advance. If well chosen, comics do not become outdated as easily as cartoons. The single picture which neither caricatures a current public figure nor is based upon a contemporary event will be classified as a comic rather than as a cartoon.

At one time, one could have spurned comic strips as something degrading, something "low-brow," something for the illiterate. Today, however, many of the more than 500 American comic strips are " ... leaning toward sophisticated satires of American life, or of humanity in general."[11]

The Basic Types of Comic Strips

In order to select good comic strips and to prepare background material, the teacher must be familiar with the basic types of comic strips. One way of categorizing them would be according to length. In this manner they can be broken down into four basic types.

1) *Totally Self-Contained.* Each panel or set of pictures is totally independent of the previous or future panel. The topic may, and usually does, vary from day to day with no formal connection. The reader need not have read the previous day's comic strip to appreciate the current one. "Beetle Bailey" or "Blondie" are representatives of this type of strip.

2) *Quasi-Self-Contained.* The panel is basically self-contained and can be understood without reference to the previous day's or the following day's strip. The comic strip artist lets the strip revolve around one topic for a number of days until the public is ready for a change or until he has virtually exhausted the possibilities of that topic. Although the reading of the previous day's strip is not necessary, it may enhance the comprehension of the reader. The creators of "Peanuts" and "B.C." often draw their strips in this manner for a number of days and then revert to the totally self-contained type for a short period.

3) *The Short Sequence.* In the short sequence, it is necessary for the reader to follow the strip for a number of days to determine the point. Often there is little humour in this type of strip, but rather, one finds a mystery, crime, or adventure story being unfolded which is supposed to maintain reader interest at a high level. Two strips which fit this category are "Dick Tracy" and "Li'l Abner."

4) *The Continuous Sequence.* In the continuous sequence there doesn't seem to be any real crisis or climax with the situation being resolved and a new sequence being started as in the shorter sequence. The reader is taken through the daily life of the characters almost without beginning or end. An example of such a strip is "Gasoline Alley," in which characters are born, grow old and die as in life itself.

It is basically the former two types that appeal universally to the youngster, to the adolescent and to the adult; to the youngster and adolescent because of the humourous superficiality and the artful drawings and to the adult on the basis of the subterranean connotations and their criticism of some aspect of society or human nature.

It would also be possible to compare comic strips to the various literary genres; the short and long sequence to the short story and the novel, and the self-contained to the poem.

A poem makes the most efficient use of a limited number of words. Each word is chosen for its maximum effectiveness. So too, the self-contained strip attempts as briefly and pregnantly as possible to depict a story with a limited amount of language, but driving home with full force that which is used. An example of such a strip is "B.C." drawn by Johnny Hart. If we look at one of his four picture panels, we can see the following:

1) The first panel depicts a cave man standing at the foot of a hill. At the top of the hill a huge boulder has broken loose and is starting to roll down the hill.

2) The second panel shows us the cave man who has become fully aware of the rock and the danger it holds for him and his tribe.

3) In the third, he is rushing homeward screaming "Rock!" with all the emotional force of danger portrayed in it.

4) In the final panel, we see his tribesmen all lined up to help him, each having recognized the danger and the immediacy of the emergency, and each with a rock in his hand.

Thus we are shown, through the misinterpretation of the one simple work "Rock," that a situation has developed which endangers the entire community and which is a very clear case of the lack of communication. This type of comic strip is the kind which is most effective in making its point and which comes the closest to being the equivalent of the political cartoon.

During the remainder of the discussion concerning comics, we shall proceed from the following definition: In spite of numerous early examples which combined drawings and language and which extended from the Gobelin tapestries in Bayeux over the church windows during the Middle Ages to the Ruppin and Munich illustrated sheets[12] — in 1806, Goya in painting the history of the bandit El Maragato probably produced the first strip in the modern sense — we consider comic strips to be a specifically American popular art which is in a state of continuous change, whose standards are based on traditional stereotypes, and which evolve from the creative impulses of individualistic caricaturists and from the indirect gyroscopic influence of the demanding and fickle readers which actually constitutes public opinion.

The Cultural Message of the Comic Strips
When Applied to Area Studies Courses

If one considers comic strips from the aspect of their use in the classroom, then one should entrust a certain amount of choice and sequence to the students since pre-selection by the teacher could reduce the motivational element of the materials. In addition, it seems essential that the teacher have a clear picture of the concepts presented and in addition be knowledgeable concerning the historical background of this stratified type of trivial literature.

The exceptionally cultural relevance of the comics becomes apparent when we consider that, according to statistical reports, the comic strips in the Sunday editions are devoured by at least 100 million Americans from all social classes, age levels, and races. Hence the largest audience of any known mass media is attracted to the same material simultaneously.[13] Since this form of entertainment has selected as its underlying themes the American family, its children and their daily life, it can readily be adopted as one source for the study of the "American way of life." To what extent problems of accessibility develop for the student learning English, shall be discussed later. At the moment, we are primarily concerned with the development of specific points of departure leading to an acquisition of cultural information.

The question of the popularity of the comic strips as they appear in newspapers, in the form of books, or as they are presented on the screen should be asked at the time one prepares to undertake an analysis of some strips. It would also be possible to use the topic of the American newspaper as a point of departure with some examples from the time of Joseph Pulitzer and his competitor William Randolph Hearst (compare Citizen Kane) and thereby trace the comics from early times to the present; especially those that still exist. Richard Felton Outcault created the series "The Yellow Kid" for Pulitzer, a strip which depicted the conditions of the New York slum area. The "Katzenjammer Kids," an American version of Max and Moritz with the background of a German immigration family, which Rudolf Dirks as an immigrant adapted for his employer Hearst, has since been drawn by many artists and is still to be found in the newspapers and in book form. (*The Katzenjammer Kids* by Joe Musial, Pocket Books USA, 95 cents.) "Dennis the Menace" and "Archie" have continued the tradition of the imaginative, mischievous youngster.[14] The things that Dennis, who is the age of his two prototypes Max and Moritz, undertakes are carried on by Archie and his adolescent high school pals.[15] Thus each age group receives "equal time" since adults are always the target of their burlesque escapades. Dennis is strikingly moderate when compared to Hans and Fritz, the *"Katzenjammer Kids."* He embodies the exact opposite of that which is referred to as the negative side of the comics. He epitomizes the baby of the family who stays close to the nest, and upon whom so much affection is showered, and to whom so much understanding is demonstrated that he cannot possibly be considered anything other than slightly mischievous. He represents the "Spoon Fed Kid" and is the product of a liberal education which allows him a voice, as a fully participating member, in the entire affairs of the family to a far greater extent than is normally the situation in Europe and other parts of the world. The family scenes show the intensive American social participation from the grill party to the formal cocktail party, from the neighborhood bridge circle to the poker parties of the local big shots. The themes of stressed manliness tied together with "keep-yourself-fit" training and of the mandatory calorie counter and the bathroom scales are characterized from the point of view of the child. We are also returned to our childhood days through the eyes of Dennis as he indulges in a hamburger at the local snack shack or as he watches a program on TV.

While Dennis pokes fun at such things as the distribution of milk in the school and at the busy work concocted by the teachers, Archie typifies the high school student who is constantly at odds with the administration represented by the high school principal "Weatherbee." Archie always seems to find the opportunity to convincingly exonerate himself at the expense of this "noble" pedagogue. Although the comic strips choose to draw upon the middle classes for their topics in the majority of instances, "Archie" also brings into play the jeunesse doré. The elegant house of a rich father turns into a playground for the students where the would-be Hippy son and the arrogant, demanding daughter conduct homework parties in the cocktail-party style of their parents. Naturally standardized tests and their consistent usage, in spite of a universal mistrust in them, play a role in "Archie" as well as in the "Katzenjammer Kids." That parents, when possible, attempt to enjoy their vacation away from the younger generation without simply abandoning them is developed along the lines of the summer camp in "Archie" and "Peanuts," with the potentially unlimited humourous possibilities.

During his reluctant stay at the summer camp, Charlie Brown's friend Linus (Peanuts) worries about the possibility that his parents might move while he is gone without informing him. Thus the author, Charles M. Schulz, takes up the theme of the constant mobility of the American (more than 20% of the American families change their residence yearly), a phenomenon which he seems to consider a handicap for the children. In the same summer camp setting, Linus quotes from Jeremiah while the campers are gathered around the campfire, "Keep your voice from weeping and your eyes from tears."[16] The absolute commandment of American society which says "keep smiling," remain optimistic, present yourself in a young, progressive manner in order to be integrated into society pays dividends for our young orator. Shy, modest Linus with his security blanket and thumb in mouth and in spite of his initial homesickness is promptly elected camp president. Thus we see the complete success of social adjustment.

The insecurity and rapid pace of living in the American daily life which helps lead to the attitude which Linus possesses offers numerous variations and possibilities for satirical and critical observations about society as well as scathing attacks on certain aspects of public life.

What particular topics are often discussed by the "little people" in Peanuts? Some of the topics which often appear in their conversations are the constantly changing make-up of the neighborhood, the job situation, social status, peaceful community life, and satisfactory schooling. Naturally the necessary insurance (life, fire or what have you) is not missing in the catalogue of daily risks. This theme is drawn upon when Snoopy's house burns down. Since he was probably guilty of smoking in bed (according to Lucy), it is his own fault. His Van Gogh and all his other treasures have been lost and with mention of a Van Gogh painting we can move to the next area of interest, namely the lack or so-called lack of cultural life, which is related to the overwhelming interest in sports at the expense of intellectual activity.

Charles Schulz (Peanuts) has labeled Schroeder, the Beethoven lover, a semi-intellectual outsider who forgets all the splendors of this world once he is settled behind the keys of his miniature grand piano and who cannot be awakened from his dreams even by marriage-happy Lucy. In "Beetle Baily," Private "Plato" takes over this role. Incidentally he appears together with Lt. Flap, one of the first Black figures to appear in one of the most widely read strips since the initiation of the self-control code against horror, brutality and racial discrimination based on the Comics Code Authority (1955).[17] Dr. Howland Owl (Pogo), a modern, psychologically-refined version of the "wise old owl" embodies less the type of sympathetic outsider such as Schroeder or Plato but much more the arrogant author and intellectual.[18] We often encounter this type of inhibited intellectual, who usually wears glasses, in entertaining films, in which a leader is shown being manipulated by or manipulating the intellectual individual who stands outside the usual boundaries of society and who is suspect of being an uncontrolled or uncontrollable, potential instigator of some type of disaster. (Note the cartoons, articles and commentaries based upon Richard Nixon's relationship to Henry Kissinger or the film Dr. Strangelove.)

The rhetorician and poet in Johnny Hart's "B.C.," on the other hand, can be considered as a thoroughly useful member of society because of his skillful capabilities as manager of the baseball team. He is a caveman and instead of a name, he has a peg-leg by which he can be recognized.

The technical vacuum alongside the civilizing, psychological, and cultural problems of the modern consumer society is not spared in the mirror of hidden critical analysis. Hence, the "wastemakers" who do not give the public all that they could are the target of a few pot shots in "B.C." and "Peanuts."

Law and Order is a natural for the slightly right-oriented Al Capp. In "Li'l Abner" we find him satirizing the poorly paid policeman (Fearless Fosdick) being beaten by a little old lady (in reality a leader of a gang à la Ma Barker) with an umbrella and then being charged with police brutality.[19]

"Pogo" written by the liberal Walter Kelly reached its high point when he attacked and denounced the Communist witch hunts during the turbulent era of Senator Joseph McCarthy. The "Pogo" strip has been slowly but definitely pushed into the background by "Peanuts," "B.C.," and other strips which have a stronger entertaining element as well as requiring less concentration in order to be understood.

The form of the presentation alongside the intellectual or semi-intellectual strip becomes more and more varied; "Mickey Rodent" in *Inside Mad*[20] is a parody of the beloved Mickey Mouse strips, in which a constant and ingenious play on words is presented, although the reader is not considered capable of catching them and so they are presented in goldface type (Darn-Old Duck). The Katzenjammer Kids have become the KatchandHammer Kids. The preoccupation of many young American readers for themes based on the First World War, which is also reflected in Peanuts in Snoopy's constant battles on his Sopwith Camel with the Red Baron (von Richthofen) is satisfied in Mad with a constant flow of bowdlerized technical terms pouring from the mouth of the jet pilot "Smilin' Melvin."

Finally the snake takes hold of its own tail (or is it tale?) in various comic strips, best represented by the cartoonist Al Capp in his series "Li'l Abner" when he draws "Fosdick." Capp points out to us that all of us, including Li'l Abner, are "hooked" on the strips. And so we find the "comic within the comic."[21]

The topical areas which would be of particular interest in the classroom could then be summed up as follows:

A. The area of American Family Life.
   1. The tension between generations at home and in school.
   2. The pampering of the children.
   3. Summer camps.
   4. Leisure time athletics and the calorie scale.
   5. Television mania.
   6. Events in the daily life of the family.

    B.   Society and the Individual
1. Code of conduct of the "successful" individual and the acceptance or rejection of the outsider.
2. Businesslife — criticism of the "wastemakers."
3. The lack of social security.
4. The lack or so-called lack of cultural orientation.
5. Preference for sports and amourous adventures compared to cultural activity.
6. Nostalgic look at the First World War and the glorification of the GI.
7. The defense of law and order.
8. The mistrust of standardized tests.

Thus, it is felt that a significant number of area study topics have been suggested which can be found at all times in many comic strips. These can be dealt with by the teacher without his becoming dependent on any specific publication. The writers of this paper do not wish to put together a methodical recipe for the selection of them but prefer to refer the readers to Ethel Tincher's rating scale. It is based on a 10-point system for the critical analysis of any comic strip.

1.	Is the drawing good?	(one point)
2.	Does the comic have complex meaning, necessitating a knowledge of what is going on in the world on the part of the reader?	(two points)
3.	If the cartoon is meant to be funny, do you laugh when you read it?	(two points)
4.	If it is a serial suspense type of cartoon or comic, do you read it every day and follow the story with interest?	(two points)
5.	Do you really enjoy the comic, or do you read it just for the sake of finding something to do? Are you able to analyze the complexity of the meaning? What connotations are there in the drawings and in the dialogue?	(three points)[22]

This chart may well serve the American teacher who is primarily concerned with developing a sense of critical evaluation in his students. For the teacher of English as a second language, it is essential to establish different guidelines for the purpose of selection. More important for English teachers are the following points:

1. Does the particular comic chosen present any aspects of American life?

2. What kinds of ideals or goals in life are approved or taken for granted?

3. What means or methods for reaching these goals are suggested?

4. What symbols and persons are condemned or rejected?

5. Can you recognize any distortion of facts, indoctrinations, or political manipulations? (Compare "Little Orphan Annie")

6. To what extent does the particular comic reflect social criticism?

7. Does it perpetuate some stereotype or cliché?

8. Which forms of simplification of problems did you find? (characters, types, slogans, prejudices, etc.)

9. Does the reader accept the "message" more easily because it is disguised in a comic strip?

10. Try to define a comic strip by using the criteria quoted above.

11. Make a comparative study of comic strips and cartoons.

12. How would you explain the fact that in some cases the comics do not make the foreigner laugh?

13. Is the text of the strip such that it can be used by the teacher in a lexical or syntactical exercise?

Although the comics certainly can be considered very attractive for the instruction of English as a foreign language, a few technical problems should not be overlooked. The accompanying vocabulary of the story in pictures is often quite limited and often comes from the area of slang or colloquialisms. The idiomatic prerequisites for simple language drills, descriptions of the pictures, or narrative interpretations do not accompany the strip and must, therefore, be most carefully prepared.

Since their inherent comical, satirical or humourous elements all reflect a certain amount of native characteristics, which are not necessarily accessible to or easily understood by the non-American, and since even somewhat simple puns do not necessarily become apparent at once, it is highly recommended that (native) English-speaking assistants or informants be consulted for necessary explanations once the texts have been selected, so that a complete understanding and immediate, spontaneous reaction can be assured when the material is introduced in class.

Footnotes

[1]Bond, F. Fraser, *An Introduction to Journalism*, The Macmillan Company, New York, 1961, p. 254.

[2]Silverman, Alvin, *The American Newspaper*, Robert B. Luce, Inc., Washington, D.C., 1964, p. 27.

[3]Bond, p. 258.

[4]White, David M. and Robert H. Abel, *The Funnies*, The Free Press of Glencoe, 1963, p. 76.

[5]Silverman, p. 26.

[6]Bond, p. 218.

[7]*The American College Dictionary*, Random House, New York, 1965, p. 185.

[8]Spencer, Dick, III, *Pulitzer Prize Cartoons*, The Iowa State College Press, Ames, Iowa, 1953, p. 140.

[9]Ibid.

[10]Ibid., p. 15.

[11]Silverman, p. 27.

[12]Hürlimann, Bettina, "Die Seifenblasensprache," *Europäische Kinderbücher in 3 Jahrhunderten*, Atlantis Verlag, Zürich und Freiburg in Breisgau, 1959, pp. 117f.
Those who wish a more detailed literary, critical analysis should refer to K. Riha, "Die Blase im Kopf in Trivialliteratur, Aufsätze Literarisches Colloquium," Berlin, 1964, pp. 176-191, or to David White and Robert Abel, *The Funnies, An American Idiom*, The Free Press of Glencoe, 1963.

[13]Metken, Günter, *Comics*, Fischer Bücherei Nr. 1120, Sept. 1970, p. 160.

[14]Ketcham, Hank, *Dennis the Menace ... Teacher's Threat*, A Fawcett Crest Book 232-01123, Greenwich, 1960, pages not numbered.

[15]*... Archie and the Generation Gap*, A Bantam Book F 5861, New York, 1970, pages not numbered.

[16]Schulz, Charles M., *The Unsinkable Charlie Brown — Peanuts*, Holt, Rinehart, and Winston, Inc., New York, 1967, pages not numbered.

[17]Metkin, p. 70.

[18]Ibid., p. 87.

[19]Op. cit.

[20]Kurtzman, Harvey, et al., *Inside Mad*, A Ballantine Book, 345.01565. "*Mad* started out three years ago as a comic book kidding only other comic strips. It has graduated today into a ... magazine, kidding not only comic strips but movies, TV, novels, commercial ads or anything it feels like.... " (Backword by Stan Freberg in 1955).

[21]Metkin, p. 74.

[22]Tincher, Ethel, "Suggestions for Evaluating Comics," *Using Mass Media in the Schools*, ed. by William D. Boutwell, Appleton-Century-Crofts, New York, 1962, p. 168.

IV

WITH WHOM?

- learning disabled students to teach left-to-right progression, discrimination of important details, comprehension of social situations, and development of a sense of humor

- deaf students for language acquisition and reading enjoyment

- intermediate and junior high students portraying their ideas on current ideas or other concerns

- ninth grade students learning about stereotyping, satire, irony, exaggeration, and incongruity while making a cartoon filmstrip

- reluctant disabled readers to stimulate an interest in reading

REMEDIATING WITH COMIC STRIPS

Phyllis N. Hallenbeck

The use of comic strips for teaching children sequencing (similar to the Picture Arrangement subtest of the WISC) and a number of other necessary skills is a relatively simple and valuable technique. Suitable comic strips can be clipped from local newspapers — with or without dialog, depending on the reading ability of the child. As an example, the teacher can divide the strip into its panels, shuffling them well, and then direct the child: "Put the pictures in order to tell a story." This method is so effective that commercially prepared sequential pictures are available for this type of training.

As another example, many learning disabled first and second grade pupils are not able to deal successfully with the Picture Absurdities items of the Binet. Comic strips may be used to remediate this deficiency also. Rather than cutting the strips into panels, the teacher can present the comic strip intact and ask the child to tell what is funny or foolish about it. It is immediately evident that these children have difficulty in grasping abstract situations, although they tend to do much better with perceptual slapstick humor. Thus, there is little difficulty in appreciating a comic strip that shows children christening a homemade raft named "Indestructible" by breaking a catsup bottle on it and then watching the raft break up and sink, the bottle remaining intact. Another readily enjoyed strip shows a man getting a parking ticket because the parking meter was hidden by a snowman which melts before the police officer appears. In another, two boys have a tug-of-war with an umbrella in the rain until it breaks and they both get wet. The child who looks at such a perceptually-based humorous strip and says he doesn't see anything funny about it does not understand what he is seeing.

This paper will discuss the relationship between the child's ability to understand what he sees and his ability to see humor in order to learn important skills. Guidance to help educators select and use cartoons appropriately is given. I shall give examples of types of comic strips for remediating various deficiencies, along with specific suggestions for their use.

Theoretical Background

There are several theories explaining humor which have relevance to remediation work with learning disabled children. Wolfenstein (1954) and Kris (1938) have emphasized the role of mastery in children's humor. The child must

Reprinted by permission of the author and the publisher from *Journal of Learning Disabilities* 9 (January 1976): 22-26.

have enough understanding of his environment for him to appreciate the humorous aspect of a particular joke situation. Wolfenstein in particular warned that humor proposed by an adult may not seem funny to children because of the mastery element.

Helmers (1965) has suggested that the purpose of children's humor is to reconfirm the "unshakeable orderliness" of the world about them. Especially in aggressive humor it is necessary for the child to distinguish the fantasy situation clearly so that he is not dismayed or made uncomfortable by it. In speaking of humor, McGhee (1971) stated:

> A reality-fantasy dimension becomes important here, in that the child perceives expectancy violations as being funny only when he has acquired a stable enough conceptual grasp of the real world that he can assimilate the disconfirmed expectancy as being only a play on reality. [p. 333]

Speaking of older children, McGhee agrees with Piaget that in the course of development the child attempts to accommodate all new stimuli into his existing schemes in a process of "reality assimilation." He further theorized that the older children are capable of "fantasy assimilation," but since accommodation does not occur with humor stimuli, the recognition of the violation of expectancy causes the humor response. "Pleasure derives from the child's certainty that the stimulus depicted does not really exist" (p. 334). Reality assimilation of humorous situations, he added, may result in interest, confusion, or fear — but not humor.

Maier (1932) advanced a Gestalt theory of humor as a sudden change and restructuring of the whole configuration, the unexpectedness of which is responsible for the humor. He stressed the importance of objectivity, believing that humor does not result if the individual identifies too closely with the situation. Bateson (1969) and Fry (1963) have suggested that reversal of figure and ground is involved in joking, as the punch line requires a sudden attention to material that has previously been in the background.

In relating these theoretical observations to the realm of learning disabilities, it becomes clear that mastery of the environment, distinguishing between reality and fantasy, objectivity (rather than egocentrism), restructuring a Gestalt pattern, and shifting readily from figure to ground and back again are all areas which may be extremely difficult for learning disabled children. This may be the explanation for their late development of a sense of humor, and/or their proneness toward the "silly" or perceptual types of humor past the age when nondisabled children have shifted to more cognitive humorous situations. It is obvious, then, that successful training of learning disabled children to appreciate comic strip humor may strengthen any or all of the above weaknesses. Some examples of the use of cartoons follow.

Encouraging Cognitive Development

As has been mentioned, slapstick or perceptual humor is most easily understood by very young or conceptually handicapped children (those who are preoperational in logic as defined by Piaget). Humor can be based on variables such as a play on words or ideas, exaggeration of the known situation, or violation of acquired expectancies (the surprise or absurd element). The last is perhaps the most frequently used by most comic strip authors. Examples are the strip in which the little girl complains she has gained six pounds in three days, causing the little boy to do some figuring, at the end of which he announces that if she keeps it up she will weigh 750 pounds in a year; or one in which a character moves a chess piece on a board and the mailman carries it off carefully while he explains that he plays chess by mail; or the professor who is explaining how flea collars work, but then comments that the trick is to get the collar on the flea.

When the cartoon is based on situations other than slapstick, much more comprehension is demanded from the reader. It has been found by researchers that there is a positive relationship between cognitive level or chronological age and complexity of cartoon situation understanding (Schaffer 1930, Zigler et al. 1966, McGhee 1971). It is also known that many learning disabled and most retarded children are late in reaching levels of logical development in keeping with their chronological age.

A first area of concern with young learning disabled children may be to distinguish clearly between fact and fantasy. Such children characteristically do not have creative imaginations, but rather tend to be very literal-minded. It may be their rootedness in the concrete which interferes with their appreciating fantasy, and the tutor or teacher may have to point out the fictional quality of the situation. "Could that really happen?"; "Could a horse really hang from a tree by its tail?"; "Could a dog really make himself look like a bird?" are questions which can be used to stimulate the perception of fantastic elements in comic strips.

Young children also tend to be egocentric in the Piagetian sense—i.e., capable of judging situations only from their own points of view. Many older learning disabled children are still captive to egocentrism, to their great social disadvantage. The quality of objectivity may be fostered by discussion of comic situations which are not enjoyed by the child because he identifies too closely. Such situations may be either aggressive or deal with supposed stupidity or constant blundering of a strip character. Aggressive themes may stir up the insecurity of the child in managing his own aggression or dealing with it from others. Stupidity themes may be too reminiscent of errors and everyday mishaps the child himself has. When these themes appear too threatening to the child, it is best to select other themes until he feels more secure.

Learning disabled children frequently have difficulty combining parts in different ways to make up whole patterns. Piaget's (1965) famous experiment with the wooden beads is often failed by older children who are not mentally flexible enough to unstring and restring the beads in their thoughts. Guiding such children to understanding cartoons that require recombining the original elements in a new way may foster this type of flexibility. For example, a strip in which the characters are involved in announcing the rules for a rope-climbing contest in which the rope is hung from the neck of a giraffe, who is concerned about the weight of the climbers; or one in which there is talk of using the sun as a source of energy, with the comment that it would take an awfully long extension cord.

Figure-ground relationships are most readily associated with the visual sense, but exist in all other modalities as well because of the attention factor. It is *what we attend to* that determines what is figure and what is background. Deliberately shifting attention from figure to ground may be quite difficult for the learning disabled because of the mental flexibility required. Working with humorous situations requiring such shifts is often helpful in developing this ability.

Some strips require an educational background that many learning disabled children (being nonreaders, etc.) do not have. This type of strip gives the opportunity to broaden the child's knowledge in a pleasant way. For example, the cartoon in which two little girls are telling the boy that the Andes Mountains are in South America and the Alps in Europe, and laughing because he wrote on his test paper that Andy's drugstore sells a sundae called Alps; or when the point of humor in the strip depends on understanding the word "topographical"; or when a penguin asks for some kind of food from his homeland and is offered an Arctic Delight (a bowl of ice cubes). Enrichment and education may thus be provided for children who, because of their difficulties, have a view of the world more limited than that of their nondisabled peers. Such children are not, by definition, retarded and therefore should be expected to acquire a normal background of knowledge. Learning from such strips is likely to be quite scattered, but can be important in the larger scheme of the child's development, in expanding his horizons and motivating him to learn more about his environment.

No matter what aspect of thinking is being tapped, comic strips are intrinsically motivating to most children. They will tolerate being taught, being explained to, being questioned, with considerable patience because they want to enjoy the humor, and because they want to be like other children. It is important for the teacher or tutor not to overdo, or require too much at a time. Difficult strips may be mixed with easier (perceptual) ones to set a comfortable pace for the pupil.

Advantages for Reading and Verbal Expression

In addition to the left-to-right sequencing the child must learn, strip dialog itself is good practice in reading for learning disabled children. Many strips are printed in all capital letters, which younger children and those with reversal problems find easier to read. For children who characteristically pay little attention to detail (and consequently read "house" for "horse," "will" for "well," etc.) there are comic strips that require noticing detail to make sense. The expression on a character's face, darkening of the sky to indicate passing time, the print on a small sign, are examples of some of the details essential to understanding certain situations. By using such cartoons the teacher or tutor is training the child to attend to small details, and should make the importance of this clear to the child. One can say, for example, "You have to notice little things like that or you miss the fun."

The symbolism of comic strips provides, in effect, a new code for dyslexic children to learn. Light bulbs over characters' heads indicating sudden ideas or understanding; very large letters in the dialog or wide-open mouths indicating yelling or shouting; use of isolated exclamation points or question marks around a character's head indicating surprise or curiosity; swirls of dust or horizontal lines demonstrating speed or movement; stars floating around for injury or pain; the conglomeration of punctuation and other marks standing for profanity are all examples of this code. It is interesting that many children must be taught what the symbols mean; they are unable to derive the meaning from the context. All of the symbols are readily learned by even the most dyslexic children, however, if the meanings are consistently pointed out. Once a child has learned comic symbolism, he can use it to entertain himself in leisure time.

When a child is asked to explain why a strip is funny, he is then exercising his "verbal expression" ability to comply. The alert teacher or tutor can help him increase his vocabulary, use good syntax, and correct pronunciation in the expression of his ideas. Just as important as good language usage is the child's ability to explain or describe something *completely*. This underlies his ability to narrate an understandable story, write a composition which hangs together, and answer future essay questions acceptably. The teacher must be unwilling to settle for a partial explanation of the situation, but must insist on a complete one, even if it is necessary to supply the missing parts for the child until he can do so himself. For instance, it is not enough for the child to say, "His father is smoking a pipe and he is getting sick." Who is getting sick and why? "The little boy is getting sick *because it smells so bad*." It is also not enough for a child to say, "The goat ate the sign and got sick," when the point of the humor is that the sign said "Slow" and the goat is saying (in the midst of his illness), "But I did eat it slow."

Paine (1974) has presented the possibility of using comic strips to teach children the use of quotation marks, among other things. Children can rewrite the dialog, putting the speech of each character inside the quotation marks with appropriate punctuation, and adding "he said." Since the speech balloon is always a direct quotation, reading comics and using them in this way can help children sort out what is direct from what is indirect quotation.

Conclusions

Some ideas have been presented here for the use of comic strips in remediation work with learning disabled children. This material is economical and almost universally available. It may be used one-to-one or made into transparencies for work with groups. A collection of strips offers opportunity for short lessons with young children who lack attention span, or longer lessons for an older, more patient child. Comics are intrinsically motivating as children want to understand the humor in order to laugh.

For remediation purposes, comic strips can be used for enrichment and incidental education in presenting facets of the world. They may be used for sequencing and better understanding of social situations. Proper choice and use can foster abstract thinking, including objectivity, reversibility of figure and ground, and restructuring whole patterns. Differentiation of fantasy and reality is implicit in comprehension of comic situations. Having the child explain completely why the strip is funny encourages good verbal expression. There are strips with dialog printed in capitals for beginning readers, and strips without any dialog for nonreaders. All strips require the left-to-right orientation, and many strips also require the noticing of small details for comprehension of the humor. Dialog may be used to teach the difference between direct and indirect quotations. Although this is not an exhaustive list of the possibilities, it suggests a new tool, or new uses for an old tool, to those working to remediate difficulties of learning disabled children.

References

Bateson, G.: "The Position of Humor in Human Communication." In J. Levine (Ed.): *Motivation in Humor*. New York: Atherton, 1969.

Fry, W. F.: *Sweet Madness: A Study of Humor*. Palo Alto, Calif.: Pacific Books, 1963.

Helmers, H.: *Sprache und Humor des Kindes*. Stuttgart, Germany: Ernest K. Verlag, 1965.

Kris, E.: "Ego Development and the Comic." *Int. J. Psychoanal.*, 1938, 19, 77-90.

Maier, N. R. F.: "A Gestalt Theory of Humor." *Brit. J. Psychol.*, 1932, 23, 69-74.

McGhee, P. E.: "Development of the Humor Response: A Review of the Literature." *Psychol. Bull.*, 1971, 76, 328-328.

Paine, C. A.: "Comics for Fun and Profit." *Learning*, 1974, 3, 86-89.

Piaget, J.: *The Child's Conception of Number*. New York: Norton, 1965.

Schaffer, L. F.: *Children's Interpretations of Cartoons (Contributions to Education, #429)*. New York: Teachers' College Press, 1930.

Wolfenstein, M.: *Children's Humor*. Glencoe, Ill.: Free Press, 1954.

Zigler, E., Levine, J., and Gould, L.: "Cognitive Processes in the Development of Children's Appreciation of Humor." *Child Develop.*, 1966, 37, 507-518.

LANGUAGE FOR THE DEAF ACCORDING TO *HENRY*

Robinette Curry Hoover

Henry is a funny little cartoon character who has been a favorite of children as well as adults for over twenty-five years. Followers of the cartoon character chuckle at the antics of the snub-nosed, pot-bellied, bald-headed youngster, who is ageless and involves himself in many thought-provoking situations and activities. There is little reading involved, for the cartoonist has chosen this medium to show that, "Silence is golden. It can also be very funny." So, except for the things that Henry writes on signs or billboards (often terribly misspelled) or the occasional words that another character might say, one just sits back and imagines the language that is going on.... That is if one has a language background.

Several years ago, as a teacher at the Eastern North Carolina School for the Deaf in Wilson, I decided to use the Henry cartoon in an attempt to encourage the use of more natural language in an almost totally manual class of young deaf children. It was my hope that the students would relate to Henry, since he, like the majority of the class did not speak, but could see, act out, write, and think.

The local newspaper carried a perfect layout of Henry in the Saturday comic section for the making of transparencies that were easily visible to the students. The pictures, in color, could then be mounted on tagboard, construction paper, or index cards and laminated to insure their safe-keeping for the teaching sessions which lay ahead. Each week, a set of transparencies and the picture cards were made for the class and put into a file for later use.

Correspondence was begun with the cartoonist, Mr. John J. Liney, Jr., of Huntingdon Valley, Pennsylvania, who had taken over at the drawing board of the late Mr. Carl Anderson, the creator of the cartoon strip character. Mr. Liney was most helpful and encouraging in those first few months of trying to improve the language lessons. He sent books, original cartoon drawings, and much love and warmth as he wrote us concerning the cartoon strip and how it had helped foreign students in their language development, as well as its many other uses in schools around the country.

A refugee school in Canada, for example, helped its students learn English by flashing enlarged pictures of Henry strips on a screen and having the group explain his actions in their new tongue. A school in Burlington, Vermont, had used Henry for reading readiness in the kindergarten and first grades. Some of their aims included:

Reprinted by permission of *American Annals of the Deaf* (December 1974, vol. 119, pp. 590-94).

1. Establishing left to right eye movement.

2. Telling a story in a logical sequence.

3. Fostering an ability to respond to picture clues.

Mr. Liney stated that since pantomime is a universal language, Henry, specifically could be read in any "foreign land." It was this particular statement that made me conscious of its potentiality in teaching language to the deaf.

It is my aim and desire that teachers who might experiment with this method of teaching will share their ideas and findings so that language according to Henry might open doors for deaf children everywhere as they find meaning and purpose in their acquisition of language.

Henry is appealing to most all of us, I think, because he does things that all of us have experienced at one time or at least have thought about doing. To a little deaf child who has not yet learned language, Henry can help translate ideas from pictures into written and oral thoughts, therefore, making language come "alive" ... bearing meaning to him personally.

In using the cartoon strip, I soon realized that all language and language principles must be presented as they come up naturally in the particular sequences. To be more specific, one can not wait until the child reaches a certain age or grade level to receive certain language principles. It must be given and explained as it comes up in the cartoon strip at the moment. Of course, the language must be modified or made more simple in the lower grades, but as the child matures, so will the language.

Henry, in all his silence, teaches language like no one else can, I believe. He makes language experience stories fun and realistic and much more understandable to the child. He develops a sense of awareness of "what's happening now" to the child who is away from home as well as for those who may live at home but often wonder why everyone is laughing or enjoying a certain situation. Most of all, Henry can help the little deaf child develop a sense of humor and curiosity and enable him to "laugh" while he is learning. He helps the deaf child who has no outward appearance of having language realize that his thoughts are like other people's thoughts and that sometimes his own ideas are more clever than his classmates and suddenly he will burst forth with ideas and creativity. Language begins to have meaning and the strange curvy lines on the chalkboard suddenly coincide with his own thoughts. This is when the child realizes that his thoughts can be translated into "words" and that by using words, he can be understood by others.

The children surprised me after only a few sessions with Henry. One day, after working during the week on a sequence involving Henry wanting to buy a watch for his girlfriend, Henrietta; a bright-eyed little girl in the class was observed while writing a letter home to her mother. She had resigned herself to the fact that the letter was half written for her on the board and all she had to do was to shape the letters onto her letter paper, when suddenly she put down her pencil and began to stare out of the window. As a teacher, one could feel the thoughts racing through her mind. She wanted to tell something, but, she did not see it written for her on the board and therefore did not know how to express it. She looked toward the desk and signed, "I want ... watch." Upon being told to "write it," she drew up her shoulders and raised her eyebrows quizzically. Her expression said, "Do you mean that if I wrote that on this paper, I might get one?" The nod from her teacher was all she needed. She picked up her pencil and smiled as she wrote "I want ... watch." This was the beginning. One small article, with little meaning to the deaf child, the article *a* was added and there it was ... a sentence ... that would be read somewhere by a mother who would make every effort to see that her wish was granted. This kind of language learning is what teachers of the deaf wait patiently for.... The kind that says "I" see a need. "I" want to learn to express "my own" thoughts. Will you help "me"? The personal need of the individual child and Henry, a silent cartoon character had been the motivator and the teacher.

In presenting the cartoon strips to various classes during the past few years, I have developed a few suggestions that may be helpful. First of all, let the child respond to the picture *before* offering *any* help at all! This is hard, but it is most important. It was found that during the experimental stages of using Henry in language classes, the teachers were doing all the thinking and creating and their ideas were not always the same as all the children's. Although this was a start and the children did respond or "parrot" back what the teacher had said or signed or written, this was not the ultimate goal and we were destroying the child's own initiative and originality almost without our knowledge.

Some of the children saw the pictures in one way, while others seemed to be focusing their attention on a totally different thought or idea. We were stilting many of the student's own clever and original ideas unintentionally. Here again, the teacher will have to take into account the maturity of the class, the language that the child already has or does not have, and other learning problems or handicaps involved. All of these things should be well thought out before presenting the cartoon to your own particular group.

Henry "sessions" might well be started by having the students just discuss the pictures in the sequence. Give each child the opportunity to give his "own" idea of what is going on in the picture. Picture cards may be used but the overhead is perfect because they can all see so much better. If picture cards are used the students can get practice in mixing up the sequence and putting it back in order. Next will come the question and answer period, perhaps, letting the children question or point out the things that "they" noticed first when they saw the particular segment. This should be done in any manner that is in some form of communication. Some will sign, some will come up with expressions that you didn't dream they knew, some will want to draw pictures on the board, others will use part-fingerspelling, signing, and gesturing, many will want to tell about similar experiences that they had "before." I can promise that all will watch and become involved.

After the discussion, the sentence work might begin. It was rare that a student would come up with a perfect sentence during those first months but we accepted what they gave and then with the help of the Fitzgerald Key, syntax charts, or other devises or crutches, we began to show how a sentence could be built from a picture and also from a mental picture in their own minds. We wanted to let the children see the language first as it evolved before their eyes from within a picture on the screen. This was the first major breakthrough for many of them and they were on their way. For others it was a slow process and much help and encouragement was needed. For a few the pictures were funny and the "signs" flew but they still did not quite relate the idea that the "writing" part had any connection to the "joy" of just looking at the pictures. Still, it was a start in the process of language development and we were proud of them all.

Some of the cartoon strips may look extremely difficult at first glance and some just don't seem interesting enough but it was found that some of the very cartoons that we almost didn't present were the ones from which language and related ideas simply "oozed" forth. The students let us know soon enough if the cartoon strip has captured their imaginations or not.

Somewhere, in an education class or in the teacher training program perhaps, we were told that one can dwell on a certain subject or project too long and destroy it for the child. So, I find it is advisable not to belabor the use of the Henry cartoon strips. Let it be a fun learning experience and when it ceases to be so, put it away for a week or so. Henry should never be made a chore but rather a time of laughing and learning together.

Because of the great volume of transparencies that can be made in only a short period of time, it was found that a central file became a necessity. The material can be filed in accordance to subject matter and made easily accessible to the teachers who are using them.

The cartoonist advises that the transparencies and any other material about Henry should carry a credit line "copyright by King Features Syndicate" or C.

KFS

It would be wonderful to have the transparencies in color but the time element became a factor in getting them ready for a class and the "plain vanilla" proved just as effective in black and white. Any ideas in improving this area would be most appreciated.

There is no doubt that excellent film strips can be made, with the proper consent from King Features Syndicate, 235 East Forty-fifth Street, New York, N.Y. 10017, or that tapes could be made on T.V. for viewing in the classrooms or in the dorms or cottages. These could be captioned or uncaptioned depending on the ways in which they will be used.

One idea was to pattern a language drill book, similar to the Croker, Jones and Pratt series, using Henry as the subject with questions and answers as well as exercises on certain language skills or principles. These however were made by the teacher and have not been perfected enough for any further comment at this time.

For language recall, a picture is flashed on the overhead screen and the children can come up to write about what is *happening* or *happens*, blacked out to remember what *happened*, and then discussions arising about what might happen in the next picture. Schools having individual overhead projectors and screens in their language and communication classes are at an advantage in that the teacher can monitor immediately the mistakes or the areas that need attention for each individual. However, even without this kind of system it is rare that a child will look at another's paper or even try to copy another's language. They all want their work to be "different" and "not the same."

Many students who had trouble with the written form of language came up with come cartoons that were so outstanding that I am sure had we taken the time to submit them to Mr. Liney he just might have used the ideas in his cartooning ventures.

Although it may seem that this material is only for primary or preschool children or those in the elementary grades, this is certainly not the case. The older students were just as "excited" to meet Henry and to use their language to tell about the series of pictures. They also showed great talent in their cartooning.

I suppose the thing that made this idea of trying to spread "Henry" to other schools for the deaf came about with an older class of surly and unexcitable students who would send up a burst of applause upon seeing the Henry transparencies being brought out for a few minutes of language "fun" where they could individually tell things like they wanted to. After-all, isn't that what language is all about!

"MEANWHILE ... ": A LOOK AT COMIC BOOKS AT ILLINOIS SCHOOL FOR THE DEAF

Bill Stark

"Odd as it seems, I would say comic books significantly contributed to my language development. I used to have stacks and stacks of comic books and traded them with hearing kids. Perhaps, subconsciously, I learned dialogue, which I consider crucial in language development. Instead of discouraging me, my parents would give me money to buy and collect classics comics, which in turn spurred me to borrow classic books from the library as I grew older." (Bowe, 1974)

The above is but one of many testimonies from deaf adults crediting their reading of comic books to have been a significant factor in their language development. It is also through comics that many deaf persons first experienced interest and enjoyment in reading.

The pictures in sequence format of comic books make them a visual form of language and thus a "natural" for use with the deaf. However, many programs for the deaf, including our own, have hesitated to use them. It wasn't until 1968 that we began very timidly and on a small scale to introduce comic books into our library and our classrooms.

Why Did It Take Us So Long?

There has long been a comic book stigma. Much of the criticism, focusing on subject matter treatment and quality of writing, is a holdover from decades ago.

In 1948, public outcry against the crime infested, sex saturated tales promoted publishers to hire censors and tone down the violence. Six years later the Comics Association of America was formed. This association, which represents 80% of the comic book industry, adopted the comics code. The comics code authority, an agency which operates apart from the comic industry, has the responsibility for enforcing the code and keeping a reign on comic book content. Reviewing comic books prior to their publication, its aim is to " ... make certain that comics are reasonably acceptable, morally, to reasonable people" (Goldwater, 1974). To receive the code's seal of approval (see figure 1 [page 148]), comic books have to adhere to strict standards concerning editorial matter,

Reprinted with permission of the author and *American Annals of the Deaf* (October 1976, vol. 121, pp. 470-77).

dialogue, costume, and treatment of subjects such as religion, race, sex, marriage, and violence.

Figure 1

COMICS CODE SEAL OF APPROVAL
Comic books which meet the comics code standards bear this
seal in the upper right hand corner of their cover.

Sex is one of the subjects which is perpetually a topic of criticism in any reading material. The comics code states that illicit sex relations are not to be portrayed, rape shall not be shown or suggested, and sexual perversion or any inference to same is strictly forbidden. The treatment of sex in comic books has been likened to the attitude toward sex in the 1950's. For example, it made national news recently when Clark Kent kissed Lois Lane. Unlike the 1950's, but consistent with our times, today's romance comics often picture a more involved and aggressive female. A boy may receive karate assistance from his girlfriend if the bully kicks sand in his face at the beach.

In respect to violence, the comics code states that no gory or gruesome crime, depravity, or excessive bloodshed shall be permitted. While there are many scenes with fist fights and earth shaking wrestling matches, bloodshed and killing are mainly shadowy suggestions even in war comics. There is never any mistaking who the heroes are in comics, and the villains always meet their just end as a result of their ill-gotten gains. Horror or terror comics, according to the comics code, must be handled in the classic tradition of Frankenstein, Dracula, and similar literary works written by Edgar Allen Poe, Conan Doyle, and other respected authors. Considering the format of comic books, they seem to be reasonably successful in achieving this goal. In comparison to movies and television, comic book treatment of violence is relatively mild.

For years there have been those who have said that comic books are vulgar and poorly written. These critics have tended to favor the preservation of literary form at the expense of substance. Characters' words spoken in overhead balloons are precise and have been more likened to a sound track than a documentation. Having the economy of a telegram, they promote imagery and realism. "Good English" out of the mouth of a comic book character caught in a catastrophic situation would be unbelievable. It is the very fact that comic books contain inventive language and slang that gives them a currency and widens their appeal to young people. Scaling the height of a tower in pursuit of a villain, Batman is suspicious of something he sees and states, "If that's a coincidence, I'm Henry Kissinger." Archie's frustration at being unable to loosen the collar of his shirt is expressed as an "expletive deleted."

What Types of Comics Do We Use at I.S.D.?

The majority of the comics we select are of the following types: classics and classics junior, animated cartoon, humor, science fiction, and teen-age adventure. To a lesser extent we chose detective, mystery, romance, war, western, and superhero types.

Most of our comic books come from the nearly 100 individual comic book titles published by major newsstand comic publishers. These publishers include Marvel Comics (world's largest), DC Comics, National Comics, Dell Comics, Gold Key, Harvey Comics, Archie Comics, King Features, Chartlon Comics, Warren Publications, Skyworld, and Classic Comics.

In addition to newsstand comics, we select a few other titles which are available from church groups and special interest groups. Alcoholics Anonymous, The American Cancer Society, The American Dental Association, and B. F. Goodrich are a few examples of publishers of special types of comics.

Several of the comic book publishers have expanded their scope. Just issued (or soon to be) are separate especially prepared comics to aid reading programs. A packet of materials on Marvel Comics' Spiderman contains a special reader, picture sequence cards, and other reading aids.

Some publishing companies have begun to copy the successful comic book format. An especially good series in that format is the *Now Age Illustrated* by Pendulum Press. This series, with vocabulary based on the Dale-Chall list, is beautifully illustrated and familiarizes the reader with great characters and stories from European and American literature.

Why Comics in Our Library?

Comics long ago infiltrated our school and were looking for a place in the library. We have comics in our library because our deaf children read them! Deaf children *want* to read them and don't have to be forced to check them out. We can only add a resounding "Amen!" to the following statement by the Orlando Public Library:

"Do we need any other justification other than the fact that kids read them? If they were reading cereal boxes, that would be the most sensible thing to fill the library with (Eisner, 1974).

To increase their life span, we have laminated all the pages and covers of Classic and Classic Junior comics. Other comics have only their front and back covers laminated. All comics are also given a special binding. Even with this treatment, comics are read and reread until they are ragged!

We have seen no evidence that the presence of comics adversely affects our book circulation. Quite the contrary. For example, our high school language arts teachers have testified that the reading of classics comics has led students to read simply written versions of the classics themselves.

In the selection of comics for the library, we follow the following guidelines: First, we are cautious not to compare comics with any other type of literature. They should be judged on their own merit. Second, we try to select those comics which are visually appealing. Third, we apply our usual selection policy considerations as set forth in the *Library Bill of Rights* of the American Library Association. These considerations include the provision of materials to enrich and support the curriculum, taking into account the varied interest, ability, and maturity levels of the students we serve. Comics are also reviewed very closely as to their treatment of subjects such as ideologies, race, religion, and sex.

School libraries can make a start on their collection by obtaining distributors' catalogs from local newsstands. Comic book publishers will often furnish lists of their titles. The Comics Code Authority, 60 East 42nd Street, New York, is an excellent source of information on comics.

Why Comics in Our Classrooms?

We have comics in our classrooms for the same reason they are in the library. Deaf children read them! Perhaps they read comic books because they are unrelated to past reading failures. Or, perhaps they are simply attracted to comics because they are pictorial and colorful.

Comics are used in our junior high school reading program as one of the non-text reading motivation materials. Students are given an opportunity to write "book reports" on the comics for extra grade points. Some of them actually do it!

Thermofax overhead transparencies have been made from the pages of certain comics. (These turn out surprisingly well!) Students then come up to the front of the class and, reading the transparencies, "act out" the roles. At times the balloons are left blank, and the students supply their own vocabulary. This is also a good opportunity for changing direct discourse to indirect and for summarizing or moralizing a story.

Comic books are replete with idioms. From Bugs Bunny wondering how to get Elmer Fudd "back down to earth" to the Hulk bemoaning the fact he is getting "punch drunk," comics afford numerous opportunities to teachers.

Comics have been used at our school to introduce deaf children to fairy tales, Aesop's fables, nursery rhymes, and classical literature. Pictorial classics and classics junior comics help children begin to understand these works of literature which are very difficult in their original form. Classic comics are themselves sometimes difficult to read, so we've produced slide series based on these comics. Writing our own language, we've produced sequential captioned slide stories. In sequential captioning, the caption is presented first, followed by the visual. (Slide copies from comics are excellent!) The teacher using such a slide series story will first project a caption and ask a student to read and interpret it (in gestures, signs, or pantomime). The teacher then projects the visual so that the class can see whether or not the caption was correctly interpreted. This visual is usually just one "frame" from the comic page. It is important that each visual actually illustrate the sentence or sentences on the preceding caption. Although a story told with sequentially captioned slides is not real "programmed instruction," it can have many things in common with a programmed lesson. First of all, the material is presented in small, logical steps. Secondly, the student has frequent opportunity to respond (to the meaning of the printed word). The student gets immediate feedback to his interpretation of the caption because the visual which follows it either does or does not confirm his interpretation. Some teachers initially voiced doubts about using sequentially captioned slides, as they were concerned that sequential captions would confuse their students. These same teachers later reported that their students were not confused at all. Several teachers even felt that students learned more by reading sequentially captioned slides than by reading traditionally captioned slides. We've been delighted to see these slide stories motivate students to read the comics themselves or simply written versions of the literary works upon which the comics are based. The "story" we write is sometimes handed out separately to students as a reading lesson (see figure 2 [page 152]).

"Meanwhile ... "

Within the limits or propriety, anything a deaf child reads is an educational tool. The assumption that reading is an end in itself is self defeating. Deaf children read material that gives them pleasure and satisfies their quest for knowledge and understanding of the world. Material like that can be found in comic books!

Figure 2

**A COMPLETION EXERCISE BASED ON THE SLIDE SERIES
STORY, "WAR OF THE WORLDS."**

WAR OF THE WORLDS

An astronomer in London, England, saw a strange thing through his telescope. A brilliant flash of gas was shooting from Mars toward the earth. When it was close to earth, it _____ like a falling star.

The meteorite (falling star) _____ in the country, just outside London. A man went to look for it. He found it. It was not a meteorite. It was a spaceship!

By nightfall, many _____ people had gathered around the spaceship. Then, a strange thing happened. The lid of the spaceship unscrewed and _____ off. A tentacle emerged. More tentacles emerged. It was a monster from Mars! There were other Martian monsters just like it.

People ran to hiding places and watched the Martians. The Martians erected a strange machine. A beam of light flickered out from the machine. The people were afraid. They _____ a white flag to show they wanted peace. Suddenly, blinding flashes of light struck at the people and the landscape! Many people were killed.

One survivor went _____ into the city of London. He told people about the Martians. They laughed at him _____ they didn't believe his strange story.

Then, other space ships came through the sky. The Martians began to attack the cities. People _____ to escape. Nothing could stop the Martians. There was no place that was really safe. Everything was _____ and desolate. Everything seemed hopeless. But, then a strange thing _____. Everything became quiet. The monsters stopped their machines. A man began looking around to see what had happened. The monsters were dead. They had been killed by some of the smallest living things on earth — germs.

tried	happened	ruined	waved	fell
looked	back	because	landed	curious

References

Bowe, Frank. The DA Interview: Dr. Allen E. Sussman. *The Deaf American*, July-August, 1974, pp. 7-11.

Eisner, Will. Comic books in the library. *Library Journal*, October 14, 1974, pp. 2703-2707.

Goldwater, John L. Americana in four colors. New York: Comics Magazine Association of America, Inc., 1974.

CARTOON KITS

Doris Miller

The cartoon can be a most effective means of making a point. Many profound ideas have made a lasting impact when expressed in a cartoon format. Your upper intermediate or junior high students may enjoy portraying their ideas on current events or other concerns through cartoons and captions.

But wait—yes, there is a rub. Even if children's artistic efforts have ever and always been treated with utter respect, there seems to come a time when groans of "But I can't draw" are heard in the land. At the same time, some of your students just seem to sketch perpetually—they can't seem to help themselves.

Try a little collaboration, cooperation, synergistic effort. Enlist the aid of student artists in making up cartoon kits. Put artists to work outlining head shapes, as well as some pages of features—eyes on one page, mouths on another, etc. (Have students try to keep features in scale with the heads, so the parts will fit together.) Another artist might draw torsos; another, arms and legs.

When the artists are satisfied that they have a sufficient variety of components, have them outline all their drawings with felt-tipped markers or flow pens. Then duplicate the prepared pages in class-size quantities. Staple the pages together and everyone can have a do-it-yourself cartoon kit that can be used over and over. Cartoon makers simply trace and combine whatever parts they select.

To introduce cartoon making, you might display and discuss some good examples from magazines and newspapers, pointing out the various aspects of life being portrayed and poked fun at. Invite students to suggest areas for cartooning, such as school, politics, family life, TV.

The cartoons themselves may also be prepared by team effort (pairs or small groups). Humorous lines for captions often come more easily through interaction.

Students who never considered cartooning may surprise themselves by turning out some really satisfying work, with the help of cartoon kits.

Reprinted by special permission of *Learning* (February 1978, vol. 6, p. 112), The Magazine for Creative Teaching. © 1978 by Pitman Learning, Inc.

A STUDENT-MADE FILMSTRIP

Doris Miller

As a culmination of a literature unit on humor, my ninth graders tried to prove to me that they had a sense of humor — the true test of which is, of course: Can you laugh at yourself? To do this, we decided to make a cartoon filmstrip in which the joke would be on them.

First, I asked the students to list ten things about teenagers that they felt would be annoying to adults or would reveal a "typical" teenage trait. Then we talked about how these ideas could be caricatured for humor or given an ironic twist so they say one thing but mean another.

Next, each student decided on one of the topics to illustrate with a cartoon or paste-up of a magazine cutout. For those who wanted to draw their own illustrations but were less artistically talented, I suggested using stick figures. Each cartoon was done on the top half of a 12-by-18 inch piece of pastel drawing paper (white paper sometimes makes a glare on the screen) so that the kids would have plenty of space to print their captions clearly. When all the cartoons were passed in, we selected those that were good enough to photograph for slides, and the best artists volunteered to do the title and end frames.

Next was the problem of the script for the soundtrack (and a wonderful chance for the class to do more writing). I hung the cartoons around the room, filling bulletin boards and all available wall space, and asked each student to choose at least five (not necessarily his or her own) for which to write dialog. Allowed only half-sheets of paper, they were forced into brevity. On a ditto sheet I had listed each of the cartoon frames, and they signed up for the frames they chose so that the editors would know who was doing what.

The script coordinators then organized all the separate frames, stapling them together for discussion and revision. After that began the process of elimination and condensation. The editors and I read to the class the various ideas for each frame, and together we decided which was best and, sometimes, how two or three ideas might be consolidated.

When our script was ready (typed and dittoed), we went through it together for casting. Everyone's voice was to be on the soundtrack, but we tested voices to determine who would be best in each scene. Next we chose two sound engineers and a sound-effects person who would be responsible for special effects and the ringing of the bell for advancing to the next frame. (I soon discovered that "special-effects" meant a window breaking, a toilet flushing, and a stampede.)

Reprinted with permission of the author and *Media and Methods* magazine (September 1975, vol. 12, p. 18).

Once the taping began, we found that last-minute ideas kept cropping up and on-the-spot revisions livened the production. Actors emerged from the unlikeliest sources, and we had gagsters galore.

This was a cooperative, total student involvement project in which the students learned stereotyping, satire, irony, exaggeration and incongruity. Our finished production runs for fifteen minutes and was a fun project as well as a learning experience. Besides the technical aspects and the writing skills required to put our show together, much patience, industry, and good nature were demanded. And, since every "Great Film" should have a sequel, we have now undertaken our next project, a humorous look at *How To Be a Teacher*. The kids proved that they can laugh at themselves. Can we?

WHERE IS DROOPY?

Ron Rainsbury

Cartoons and cartoon characters are great favorites among children. Why not use this interest in the classroom! Sixth graders at Washington School in Eugene, Oregon, were introduced to the rectangular coordinate system with a game—and the object of the game was to locate Droopy, a cartoon canine.

A grid for the game was drawn with a felt marker on a sheet of butcher paper and placed on a bulletin board in the classroom. The x-axis and the y-axis were both plainly marked, with positive and negative (signed) numbers on each. A student's sketch of Droopy served as a movable marker.

Before reaching this point of an introduction to the coordinate system, the students had had many experiences in using the number line. They were able to locate both positive and negative numbers and to operate with them. With these prerequisite experiences, the transition to the coordinate system was relatively easy.

With the teacher asking guiding questions, the grid on the board was used to explain the structure of the coordinate system. The positive numbers were

Reprinted from the *Arithmetic Teacher*, April 1972, copyright © 1972 by the National Council of Teachers of Mathematics.

indicated, going to the right of zero (the origin) and up. And the negative numbers were located, going to the left of zero and down.

Figure 1

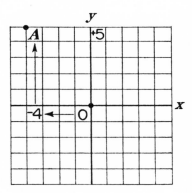

A set of coordinates was written on the blackboard: (-4, +5). Students learned that the first number of the ordered pair is found by using the *x*-axis and the second number by using the *y*-axis. Thus the ordered pair was located. See figure 1. It was evident that numbers might be plotted on lines parallel to the *x* and *y* axes.

The coordinates of five more points were then written on the board for practice:

B. (+2, +1)
C. (+3, -3)
D. (+5, +3)
E. (-2, -2)
F. (-6, -3)

The points named by these pairs or coordinates were located on the chart and the positions of these points were plotted as shown in figure 2 [page 158]. Attention was called to the fact that the points were located in all four quadrants. The word *quadrant* now became part of the students' mathematical vocabulary, along with *coordinate, ordered pair,* and others.

The students were now ready to move their cartoon favorite around and to challenge each other with the question "Where is Droopy?" One student went to the chart and placed the sketch of Droopy over a particular point. The class then had to determine the proper coordinates. Figure 3 [page 158] shows the first position.

Figure 2

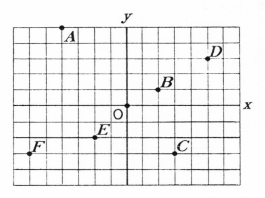

Figure 3

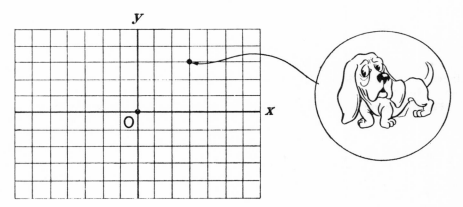

Various responses came from the class—($^+2$, $^+2$), ($^+3$, $^+2$)—and then the correct response, ($^+3$, $^+3$). The student with the right answer took his place at the chart and moved Droopy's picture to a different location.

After considerable experience with this game, students showed, by locating other points using graph paper, that they understood the basic concepts presented in the game. They were then asked to draw both x and y axes on one-fourth-inch graph paper and label the points along both axes.

The points they were to plot next corresponded to the locations of stars in one of the constellations about which they had recently learned as a part of their science instruction. They were told that if they located the points correctly, one of the following three constellations would emerge on their paper: Gemini, Cancer, or Scorpius. The coordinates given to them were: ($^+4$, $^+4$) ($^+3$, 0) ($^+6$, $^+3$)

($^+$1, $^-$2) ($^+$6, $^-$3) ($^+$7, 0) ($^-$1, $^-$4) ($^-$3, $^-$5) ($^-$5, $^-$5) ($^-$6, $^-$3). When the above data were plotted, the student could determine that the constellation was Scorpius, though not all the stars in Scorpius were included.

Throughout the lesson the importance of precision was emphasized, as well as neatness in placing the symbols. These activities proved to be very enjoyable to the class, as they found it exciting to go from the unknown to the known when plotting data. Perhaps equally important, the involvement of Droopy served as a motivator; he thus played an important role in the development of the students' understanding of the rectangular coordinate system, a prerequisite for later mathematical experiences.

THE COMIC STRIP IN THE CLASSROOM
FOR THE RELUCTANT DISABLED READER

Gary Wright

One of the contemporary problems faced by many reading and English teachers is that of the reluctant-disabled reader. There is no precise figure as to the number of students who are reading significantly below their intellectual and linguistic potential. Harris and Sipay (1975) reported that the frequency of reading disability in the United States ranges between 10 and 15 percent of the student population. If this percent is accurate, then there are millions of elementary and secondary students who are not coping with traditional classroom basal readers, literature anthologies and content area textbooks.

It is the responsibility of reading and English teachers to help motivate students to read. Often the nature of classroom reading materials is such that they do not aid the teacher in making reading an exciting, useful activity for students. Use of newspaper comic strips in the classroom may stimulate an interest in reading. There are several reasons why the comic strip could prove to be a viable source of classroom reading material.

Interest in the Comic Strip

The first American comic strip, Yellow Kid, greeted the readers of Hearst's New York *Journal* on October 18, 1896. Today it is estimated that there are 100 million Sunday comic strip readers, 90 million of whom follow the comics daily (Couperie and Horn, 1973).

Dechant and Smith (1977) noted in their review of reading interest research that comic type reading materials are very popular with primary, intermediate and junior high age students. Witty (1949) reported on a survey of 1,945 children in which 85 percent ranked the comic section of the newspaper as their favorite. Norvell (1973) questioned young people about their interests in a variety of activities. Three thousand six hundred young people between the ages of 9 and 18 participated in the survey. Children in grades 4 through 9 preferred comic strip and comic book reading over all other kinds of reading activities. Young people in grades 10 through 12 ranked comic strip reading as third in preference below magazine articles and short stories. Norvell found that interest in comic strip reading declines in the adult years. However, 48 percent of the adult college

Reprinted by permission of the author and Project Innovation from *Reading Improvement* 16 (Spring 1979): 13-17.

graduates surveyed indicated that they had maintained an interest in reading newspaper comic strips.

Comic reading material which is highly valued by young people, should not be overlooked by reading and English teachers. Such material, if used wisely with reluctant-disabled readers may lead to a maturing of reading interests and to an introduction into the world of books.

Accessibility of Comic Strips

Teachers and students alike have to look neither hard nor long to find comic strips. They are as near as the local newspaper. Delury (1977) has reported that there are 1,630 English language daily newspapers and 602 Sunday newspapers. Five major news syndicates distribute 300 different comic strips, some of which are featured in each newspaper (Horn, 1976).

The average circulation figure for daily newspapers is 60,230,329, and the average circulation figure for sunday newspapers is 50,360,000 (Delury, 1977). These figures indicate that the comic section of the newspaper is available to millions of children across the nation. The classroom teacher has only to request, and he will be inundated with daily and Sunday comic sections brought to school by his students.

Readability of Comic Strips

References to the easy reading level of comic strips is often made in the literature. However, there have been no readability studies made of comic strips. This writer has conducted a preliminary study concerning the readability levels of 20 popular comic strips.

Salituri's (1978) research indicated the following comic strip titles to be some of the most popular because of the number of newspapers across the nation which feature these strips: Peanuts, Blondie, Wizard of Id, Beattle Bailey, Dennis the Menace, Crock, Hagar, B.C., Mary Worth, Rex Morgan, Snuffy Smith, Prince Valiant, Judge Parker, Funky Winkerbean, Apartment 3-G, Dick Tracy, Steve Canyon, Tiger, Steve Roper and Ziggy.

Table 1 [page 162] presents the estimated readability of these strips. The extended Fry Readability Table (Fry, 1977), and the Maginnis extended Fry Readability Table (Maginnis, 1969) were used for the readability estimates. Three samples, each one hundred words in length were taken from the comic strips listed.

The readability estimates contained in Table 1 indicate that the comic strips analyzed have an average readability ranging from 1.8 grade level to 7.2 grade level. One-third of the comic strips in Table 1 had an average readability level below third grade. Seven-tenths of the comics had a readability level below fourth grade. The data tends to support the viewpoint that comic strips provide easy reading.

Table 1

READABILITY LEVELS OF 20 COMIC STRIPS

	Comic Strip	Sentences	Syllables	Readability	Average
1.	Apartment 3-G	15.0	130	2.7	2.7
		16.0	130	2.6	
		12.1	125	2.9	
2.	B.C.	13.5	112	1.8	3.0
		11.0	140	5.5	
		21.0	122	1.8	
3.	Beetle Bailey	15.2	116	1.8	2.2
		18.0	128	2.0	
		17.1	134	2.9	
4.	Blondie	9.0	130	4.9	3.9
		12.9	133	3.4	
		15.5	135	3.4	
5.	Crock	14.0	152	7.5	5.0
		14.0	131	3.2	
		17.0	147	4.3	
6.	Dennis the Menace	18.5	120	1.8	1.8
		20.0	120	1.7	
		15.0	125	2.1	
7.	Dick Tracy	15.6	125	2.1	3.8
		15.0	120	2.7	
		10.3	142	6.5	
8.	Funky Winkerbean	7.6	129	5.5	3.7
		11.6	124	3.0	
		9.6	114	2.7	
9.	Hagar	15.9	141	3.9	2.5
		23.0	120	1.7	
		17.7	121	1.8	
10.	Judge Parker	13.0	120	2.1	2.9
		12.3	133	3.5	
		10.2	121	3.1	
11.	Mary Worth	13.5	143	4.7	5.2
		11.5	147	7.1	
		12.5	134	3.7	
12.	Peanuts	13.5	136	3.7	3.7
		13.1	136	3.7	
		9.0	122	3.6	

Table 1 (cont'd)

	Comic Strip	Sentences	Syllables	Readability	Average
13.	Prince Valiant	9.3	143	7.0	6.9
		7.5	146	7.7	
		7.3	129	6.0	
14.	Rex Morgan, M.D.	14.0	126	2.6	3.6
		9.3	133	5.1	
		10.0	129	3.9	
15.	Snuffy Smith	11.0	134	4.4	4.4
		9.3	130	4.9	
		10.0	129	3.9	
16.	Steve Canyon	8.0	132	6.0	6.0
		10.0	132	4.5	
		6.0	137	7.5	
17.	Steve Roper	10.5	144	7.1	5.4
		10.0	131	4.7	
		10.6	131	4.3	
18.	Tiger ...	21.0	119	1.7	1.8
		15.0	123	2.0	
		11.0	123	1.8	
19.	Wizard of Id	13.0	130	3.2	2.1
		15.3	119	1.8	
		16.8	130	2.4	
20.	Ziggy	11.3	136	4.5	3.4
		15.1	132	2.8	
		15.3	133	2.8	

Readability levels of certain comic strips are low enough that the comics could prove useful in motivating and providing reading practice for reluctant-disabled readers. Many reluctant-disabled readers seem to be reading comics already. Such reading activity should be encouraged until reading proficiency has been attained. At that time, the teacher can work on expanding each student's reading tastes.

Conclusion

Burton (1961) and Murphy (1961) have provided evidence as to the positive effects comic strips have on childrens' reading habits in the classroom. Haugaard

(1973) and Alongi (1974) have attested to the literary merits of comics. Zintz (1978) has described corrective reading activities involving the use of comic strips. Fader and McNeil (1968) have stated that to hook reluctant-disabled readers on books, the teacher needs to resort to using newspapers, magazines and paperbacks in the classroom. Comic strips are found in newspapers. There are comic magazines and paperbacks which feature comic strips.

This writer has suggested that newspaper comic strips are a media which are valued by children, accessible to the classroom, and easy to read. Because of these factors, the classroom reading and English teacher should consider the potential of this media in stimulating reading interests among reluctant-disabled readers.

References

Alongi, C. V. Response to Kay Haugaard: Comic books revisited. *The Reading Teacher*, 1974, 27, 801-803.

Burton, D. L. Campaigning to get students to read. In M. J. Weiss (Ed.), *Reading in the secondary schools*. New York: The Odyssey Press, 1961.

Couperie, P., and Horn, M. *A history of the comic strip*. New York: Crown Publisher, 1973.

Dechant, E. V., and Smith, H. P. *Psychology in teaching reading* (2nd ed.). New Jersey: Prentice-Hall, 1977.

Delury, G. E. (Ed.). *The World Almanac and Book of Facts*. New York: Newspaper Enterprises Associates, 1977.

Fader, D. N., and McNeil, E. B. *Hooked on books: Program and proof*. New York: Berkley Publishing Corp., 1968.

Fry, E. Fry's readability graph: Clarifications, validity and extension to level 17. Journal of Reading, 1977, 21, 242-251.

Harris, A. J., and Sipay, E. R. *How to increase reading ability* (6th ed.). New York: David McKay, 1975.

Haugaard, K. Comic books: Conduit to culture? *The Reading Teacher*, 1973, 27, 54-55.

Horn, M. (Ed.). *The World Encyclopedia of Comics*. New York: Chelsea House Publishers, 1976.

Maginnis, G. H. The readability graph and informal reading inventories. *The Reading Teacher*, 1969, 22, 516-518; 559.

Murphy, G. E. Some start with comics. In M. J. Weiss (Ed.), *Reading in the secondary schools*. New York: The Odyssey Press, 1961.

Norvell, G. W. *The reading interests of young people*. East Lansing, Michigan: Michigan State University Press, 1973.

Salituri, J. Comic strip printing—an overview. *The Buyer's Guide for Comic Fandom*, September 8, 1978, pp. 52-54.

Witty, P. *Reading in modern education.* Boston: D. C. Heath and Company, 1949.

Zintz, M. V. *Corrective reading* (3rd ed.). Dubuque, Iowa: Wm. C. Brown Company, 1977.

BIBLIOGRAPHY

Abel, Bob, ed. *The American Cartoon Album.* New York: Dodd, Mead & Co., 1974. OP
  The editor has taken a thematic, pictorial look at cartoon humor "reflecting the American [as] seen by its cartoonists."

Arlin, Marshall, and Roth, Garry. "Pupils' Use of Time While Reading Comics and Books." *American Educational Research Journal* 15, #2 (Spring 1978): 201-216.
  The authors report on their research procedures and findings with 42 pupils in grade 3 who read either comics or books under free-reading conditions for 20 minutes a day over a 10-week period. Two factors were studied: time-on-task and time-on-reading in relation to attitude and comprehension.

Auman, L. Charles. *How Dollars Make Cents: Teacher's Guide and Student Materials.* Easton, KS: Project Consumer Operations Survival Training, 1979. 66p. (ED 190 411, EDRS.)
  This unit provides secondary school students with methods for comparative shopping of savings institutions. It contains both student materials and teacher's guide and is designed for individualized instruction. Activities include analyzing cartoons, defining the terms "savings" and "interest," and listing long-term and short-term reasons for saving money. The activities are presented in dialogue form with cartoon illustrations.

Berger, Arthur A. *The Comic-Stripped American.* New York: Walker, 1973. OP
  The author examines how the comics reflect the values of American society. The book is divided into three parts: "The Innocents"; "The Modern Age Comics"; and "The Age of Confusion."

Bloom, Grace E. *Cartoons and Comic Strips in the English as a Second Language Class.* New York: Hunter College (MA Thesis), 1979. 60p. (ED 176 559, EDRS.)
  This essay deals with the use of cartoons and comic strips to teach English as a second language. It illustrates, through past professional literature written on the subject and through specific lessons, the various instructional uses to which

cartoons and comic strips lend themselves. Cartoons and comic strips can be applied to the following language skills: structure, reading, vocabulary development, listening comprehension, culture, and writing. Examples of various cartoons and comic strips are included with activities designed to teach the various language skills.

Burns, Mal. *Comix Index: The Directory of Alternative British Graphic Magazines, 1966-1977.* Brighton, Sussex: John L. Noyce, 1977. OP
    The guide is a record of the British underground comics publishing. It contains alphabetical listings of artists, cross-references to titles with dates and publishers, and a directory of publishers. A history and chronology of publishing are also included.

"Cartoons and Comic Strips." Circular R44. Copyright Office, Library of Congress, Washington, DC 20559. June 1981. [LC 3.4/2:44/3]
    An explanation of the copyright law as it applies to comics and cartoons is given as well as how to obtain registration of collections and original materials.

Chitayat, Deanna. *The Sex Equity Pamphlet.* New York: Institute for Research and Development in Occupational Education / New York State Education Department / Office of Occupational and Continuing Education, 1980. 30p. (ED 194 218, EDRS.)
    This report on comic books, designed to overcome sex stereotyping in elementary school children by exposing them to new role models, includes: 1) a discussion of sex-role learning, stereotyped sex-role characteristics, and comic books; 2) summaries of the story lines of three comic books developed to depict new role models; 3) a black and white copy of the comic book drawings and captions for the three stories; 4) a copy of a teacher's guide and lesson plans for discussion of the three comics; and 5) an anecdotal report of a field test of the comics with a fifth grade classrooom.

Cleave, Alan. *Cartoon Animation for Everyone.* New York: Internal Publications Service, 1973.
    For those individuals interested in making cartoon characters "come alive," the author discusses animation techniques, such as planning, production, special effects, and making a cartoon movie with full sync sound.

Comic Art Collection. Special Collections, Mighigan State University Libraries, East Lansing, MI 48824.
    The Special Collections branch of the Michigan State University Libraries houses the Comic Art Collection—a collection of the superhero comics of the 1960s to present. In 1975 Randall W. Scott produced *A Subject Index to Comic Books and Related Material* based on the holdings of this collection and intended as an aid in the use and acquisition of comic art material.

Couperie, P., and Horn, M. *A History of the Comic Strip*. New York: Crown, 1973. OP

The authors have written a detailed historical account of the origins and development of the comic strip from Europe to present day. Also discussed are such topics as "the comic-strip audience," "narrative technique," "esthetics and signification," and "narrative figuration."

Gifford, Denis. *The British Comic Catalogue, 1874-1974*. Westport, CT: Greenwood, 1976.

The aim of the publication is "to list the title of every comic published in Great Britain." The author/compiler provides the user with an introduction for background and notes on using the catalog. The volume is an alphabetical listing of titles with full bibliographic details. It concludes with a cross-index of comic artists.

Guthrie, John T. "Research Views: Comics." *Reading Teacher* 32 (December 1978): 376-78.

The author poses a number of questions regarding the uses of comics in the classroom. The Arlin and Roth research project is discussed.

Hatfield, Jean. *Linda and Larry in Lillipopland: Teacher's Guide and Student Material*. Easton, KS: Consumer Operations Survival Training, 1980. 60p. (ED 190 453, EDRS.)

A unit on manufacturing and consumerism for fourth grade social studies classes is presented. The unit, organized around a learning center approach, is composed in story form with cartoon illustrations. Objectives are to define the terms consumer, producer, goods, services, resources, and labor; explain what manufacturing is; and describe the steps of the manufacturing process.

Heitzmann, William Ray. *50 Political Cartoons for Teaching U.S. History*. Portland, ME: Walch, 1975.

The book is a collection of 50 political cartoons by famous American cartoonists depicting events and issues from 1754 through 1960. Each cartoon is reproduced on 8½x11-inch paper with background information, suggestions for classroom use, and discussion questions.

Hirsh, Michael, and Loubert, Patrick. *The Great Canadian Comic Book*. Toronto, Ontario: Peter Martin Associates, 1971. OP

The authors survey the historical development of the comic book in Canada. Black and white and color illustrations are used throughout the volume.

Horn, Maurice, ed. *The World Encyclopedia of Cartoons*. 2 vols. New York: Gale Research/Chelsea, 1980.

The text, in two volumes, claims to be "the first book to survey on an international scale the entire cartoon field" and provides the user with an "overview of all the cartooning arts ... for the past 200 years." Twenty-two contributors wrote the 1,200 alphabetical entries that form the core of the encyclopedia. Illustrations accompany the text.

Horn, Maurice, ed. *The World Encyclopedia of Comics.* New York: Chelsea, 1976.
    This is a standard reference work with a short history of comics, followed by a yearly chronology, and an article on the aesthetics of the comic form by the editor. The main section contains an alphabetical arrangement of author and title entries with black and white illustrations for many of the entries and a 62-page color section in the middle of the volume. The volume concludes with a history of newspaper syndication, a glossary of terms, a selective bibliography, notes on contributors, and appendices.

Kempkes, Wolfgang, ed. *International Bibliography of Comics Literature.* 2nd ed. New York: Bowker, 1973. OP
    The bibliographer has attempted to provide an international guide to the literature relating to comics in newspapers and magazines. The volume consists of eight sections: forerunners and developmental history of comic series; structure of comics; technical aspects; readership; effects; uses for educational purposes; use in related forms of expression; and judicial and other limiting measures against comics. Two indexes are included: one of authors and the other of comic series, figures, and the artists.

King Features. Education Division, Department 1344, 235 East 45th Street, New York, NY 10017. (212) 682-5600.
    The publisher has produced a number of comic programs for the consumer to use in the elementary classroom: "Comics Math"; "Comics Reading"; "Career Awareness Program"; "King Classics Library"; and "Spanish-English Program."

Lee, Stan. *Origins of Marvel Comics.* New York: Simon & Schuster, 1974.
    The author provides a historical accounting of the development of Marvel Comics from the origins to 1974. Color illustrations are throughout the volume.

Overstreet, Robert M., ed. *Comic Book Price Guide.* New York: Harmony Books, 198- .
    Limited to American comic books, the guide, updated irregularly, places monetary value on specific comic titles. The reference work is primarily of value for collectors but also contains numerous articles and color illustrations of possible interest to the general reader, such as "A Chronology of the Development of the American Comic Book"; "How to Start Collecting Comic Books"; and "Comic Book Collections Listed."

Reitberger, Reinhold, and Fuchs, Wolfgang. *Comics: Anatomy of a Mass Medium.* Boston, MA: Little, Brown and Co., 1971. OP
    Of value primarily for its reference materials, the volume would make for interesting reading on such topics as "Super-heroes," "Criticism and Censorship," "Society as Portrayed in Comics," and "Trends and Developments."

Richardson, John Adkins. *The Complete Book of Cartooning.* Englewood
  Cliffs, NJ: Prentice-Hall, 1977.
  The author provides the user with a "complete" overview of methodology
and styles for cartooning. The volume would be most useful as a reference text
for either the beginner or advanced enthusiast.

Robinson, Jerry. *The Comics: An Illustrated History of Comic Strip Art.*
  New York: Putnam's, 1974. OP
  The author gives a detailed historical view of the origins of the American
comic strip and the cartoonists who have commented on society through their
strips.

Ross, Al. *Cartooning Fundamentals.* New York: Stravon Educational, 1977.
  The author/cartoonist discusses and illustrates activities which will assist the
entry-level artist to master sound cartooning fundamentals. A sampling of
chapters includes figure drawing, anatomy, doodling, sketching, caricature,
composition, and materials needed.

Spiderman Reading Motivation Kit. New York: McGraw-Hill, n.d.
  The kit contains six color sound filmstrips with cassettes, one action poster,
three sets of story cards, seven comic book readers, and a teacher's guide. It is
intended for use with an interest level of 9-12 and a reading level of 2-3. The
multimedia remedial program is based on original adventures by one of
America's most popular comic book and TV figures — Spiderman.

Thomas, Frank, and Johnston, Ollie. *Disney Animation: The Illustration of
  Life.* New York: Abbeville, 1981.
  The authors have chronicled the development of the characters that have
made the Disney industry famous. The volume contains numerous color and
black and white illustrations interspersed with the text. In addition to the
overview of the historical development of the company, a detailed analysis is
given of the procedures for making an actual animated movie.

Thompson, Don, and Lupoff, Dick, eds. *The Comic-Book Book.* Carlstadt,
  NJ: Rainbow, 1978.
  The text is a collection of articles by well-known writers/historians on the
development of the comic book and specific superheroes.

White, David M., and Abel, Robert M. *The Funnies: An American Idiom.*
  London: Collier-Macmillan, 1963. OP
  The authors explore the question: "What do the comic strips tell us about
American culture?" in this compilation of articles by British and American
writers.

APPENDIX

Code of the Comics Magazine
Association of America, Inc.

Originally adopted in 1954, and revised in 1971 to meet contemporary standards of conduct and morality, the enforcement of this Code is the basis for the comics magazine industry's program of self-regulation.

PREAMBLE

The comics magazine, or as it is more popularly known, the comic book medium, having come of age on the American cultural scene, must measure up to its responsibilities.

Constantly improving techniques and higher standards go hand in hand with these responsibilities.

To make a positive contribution to contemporary life, the industry must seek new areas for developing sound, wholesome entertainment. The people responsible for writing, drawing, printing, publishing and selling comic books have done a commendable job in the past, and have been striving toward this goal.

Their record of progress and continuing improvement compares favorably with other media. An outstanding example is the development of comic books as a unique and effective tool for instruction and education. Comic books have also made their contribution in the field of social commentary and criticism of contemporary life.

Members of the industry must see to it that gains made in this medium are not lost and that violations of standards of good taste, which might tend toward corruption of the comic book as an instructive and wholesome form of entertainment, will not be permitted.

Therefore, the Comics Magazine Association of America, Inc. has adopted this Code, and placed its enforcement in the hands of an independent Code Authority.

Reprinted by permission of Comics Magazine Association of America, Inc., Suite 1807, 60 East 42nd Street, New York, NY 10165.

Further, members of the Association have endorsed the purpose and spirit of this Code as a vital instrument to the growth of the industry.

To this end, they have pledged themselves to conscientiously adhere to its principles and to abide by all decisions based on the Code made by the Administrator.

CODE FOR EDITORIAL MATTER

General Standards – Part A

1. Crimes shall never be presented in such a way as to promote distrust of the forces of law and justice, or to inspire others with a desire to imitate criminals.

2. No comics shall explicitly present the unique details and methods of a crime, with the exception of those crimes that are so far-fetched or pseudo-scientific that no would-be lawbreaker could reasonably duplicate.

3. Policemen, judges, government officials and respected institutions shall not be presented in such a way as to create disrespect for established authority. If any of these is depicted committing an illegal act, it must be declared as an exceptional case and that the culprit pay the legal price.

4. If crime is depicted it shall be as a sordid and unpleasant activity.

5. Criminals shall not be presented in glamorous circumstances, unless an unhappy end results from their ill-gotten gains, and creates no desire for emulation.

6. In every instance good shall triumph over evil and the criminal punished for his misdeeds.

7. Scenes of excessive violence shall be prohibited. Scenes of brutal torture, excessive and unnecessary knife and gun play, physical agony, gory and gruesome crime shall be eliminated.

8. No unique or unusual methods of concealing weapons shall be shown, except where such concealment could not reasonably be duplicated.

9. Instances of law enforcement officers dying as a result of a criminal's activities should be discouraged, except when the guilty, because of their crime, live a sordid existence and are brought to justice because of the particular crime.

10. The crime of kidnapping shall never be portrayed in any detail, nor shall any profit accrue to the abductor or kidnapper. The criminal or the kidnapper must be punished in every case.

11. The letters of the word "crime" on a comics magazine cover shall never be appreciably greater in dimension than the other words contained in the title. The word "crime" shall never appear alone on a cover.

12. Restraint in the use of the word "crime" in titles or subtitles shall be exercised.

General Standards — Part B

1. No comic magazine shall use the word horror or terror in its title. These words may be used judiciously in the body of the magazine.*

2. All scenes of horror, excessive bloodshed, gory or gruesome crimes, depravity, lust, sadism, masochism shall not be permitted.

3. All lurid, unsavory, gruesome illustrations shall be eliminated.

4. Inclusion of stories dealing with evil shall be used or shall be published only where the intent is to illustrate a moral issue and in no case shall evil be presented alluringly nor so as to injure the sensibilities of the reader.

5. Scenes dealing with, or instruments associated with walking dead, or torture shall not be used. Vampires, ghouls and werewolves shall be permitted to be used when handled in the classic tradition such as Frankenstein, Dracula and other high calibre literary works written by Edgar Allen Poe, Saki (H. H. Munro), Conan Doyle and other respected authors whose works are read in schools throughout the world.

6. Narcotics or Drug addition shall not be presented except as a vicious habit.

   Narcotics or Drug addiction or the illicit traffic in addiction-producing narcotics or drugs shall not be shown or described if the presentation:

   (a) Tends in any manner to encourage, stimulate or justify the use of such narcotics or drugs; or

   (b) Stresses, visually, by text or dialogue, their temporarily attractive effects; or

   (c) Suggests that the narcotics or drug habit may be quickly or easily broken; or

   (d) Shows or describes details of narcotics or drug procurement, or the implements or devices used in taking narcotics or drugs, or of the taking of narcotics or drugs in any manner; or

   (e) Emphasizes the profits of the narcotics or drug traffic; or

   (f) Involves children who are shown knowingly to use or traffic in narcotics or drugs; or

   (g) Shows or implies a casual attitude towards the taking of narcotics or drugs; or

---

*The Board of Directors has ruled that a judicious use does not include the words "Horror" or "Terror" in story titles within the magazine.

(h) Emphasizes the taking of narcotics or drugs throughout, or in a major part, of the story, and leaves the denouement to the final panels.

General Standards — Part C

All elements or techniques not specifically mentioned herein, but which are contrary to the spirit and intent of the Code, and are considered violations of good taste or decency, shall be prohibited.

DIALOGUE

1. Profanity, obscenity, smut, vulgarity, or words or symbols which have acquired undesirable meanings — judged and interpreted in terms of contemporary standards — are forbidden.

2. Special precautions to avoid disparaging references to physical afflictions or deformities shall be taken.

3. Although slang and colloquialisms are acceptable, excessive use should be discouraged and wherever possible good grammar shall be employed.

RELIGION

1. Ridicule or attack on any religious or racial group is never permissible.

COSTUME

1. Nudity in any form is prohibited. Suggestive and salacious illustration is unacceptable.

2. Females shall be drawn realistically without undue emphasis on any physical quality.

MARRIAGE AND SEX

1. Divorce shall not be treated humorously nor represented as desirable.

2. Illicit sex relations are not to be portrayed and sexual abnormalities are unacceptable.

3. All situations dealing with the family unit should have as their ultimate goal the protection of the children and family life. In no way shall the breaking of the moral code be depicted as rewarding.

4. Rape shall never be shown or suggested. Seduction may not be shown.

5. Sex perversion or any inference to same is strictly forbidden.

CODE FOR ADVERTISING MATTER

These regulations are applicable to all magazines published by members of the Comics Magazine Association of America, Inc. Good taste shall be the guiding principle in the acceptance of advertising.

1. Liquor and tobacco advertising is not acceptable.

2. Advertisement of sex or sex instruction books are unacceptable.

3. The sale of picture postcards, "pin-ups," "art studies," or any other reproduction of nude or semi-nude figures is prohibited.

4. Advertising for the sale of knives, concealable weapons, or realistic gun facsimiles is prohibited.

5. Advertising for the sale of fireworks if prohibited.

6. Advertising dealing with the sale of gambling equipment or printed matter dealing with gambling shall not be accepted.

7. Nudity with meretricious purpose and salacious postures shall not be permitted in the advertising of any product; clothed figures shall never be presented in such a way as to be offensive or contrary to good taste or morals.

8. To the best of his ability, each publisher shall ascertain that all statements made in advertisements conform to fact and avoid misrepresentation.

9. Advertisement of medical, health, or toiletry products of questionable nature are to be rejected. Advertisements for medical, health or toiletry products endorsed by the American Medical Association, or the American Dental Association, shall be deemed acceptable if they conform with all other conditions of the Advertising Code.

THE COMICS CODE AUTHORITY

The Code Authority of the Comics Magazine Association of America, Inc. was established at the same time the Code was adopted, to ascertain compliance with the terms of the Code. It is headed by a Code Administrator, who has no connection with any publisher, and who exercises independent judgment to determine whether the material intended for publication meets Code standards.

Publisher-members of the CMAA are required to submit their original text and art-work to the Code Authority, *in advance of publication.* The staff carefully checks each panel of art and every line of text, ordering such changes or deletions as in the judgment of the Administrator violates any tenet or the overall principle of the Code. Being an industry self-regulation program, the publisher may appeal the decision of the Administrator to the CMAA's Board of Directors, but in nearly two decades of operation, this privilege has been rarely used. In almost every instance, the decision of the Administrator has prevailed.

Finally, each individual page must receive the stamp of approval of the Code Authority, or authorization from the Board of Directors, before the publisher may place the official Seal of Approval on the upper right-hand portion of the comics magazine's cover.

INDEX

Compiled by Olga B. Wise